The Chihuahua

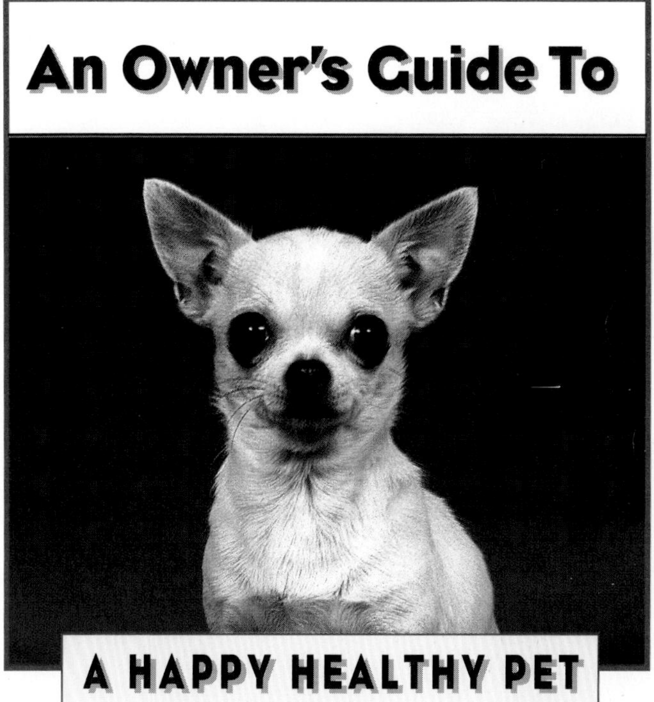

Howell Book House

Howell Book House
A Simon & Schuster Macmillan Company
1633 Broadway
New York, NY 10019

Library of Congress Cataloging-in-Publication Data
Terry, E. Ruth, 1927–
The chihuahua: an owner's guide to a happy healthy pet / E. Ruth Terry.
p. cm.

ISBN 0-87605-493-9

1. Chihuahua dogs. I. Title
SF429.C45T46 1996
636.7'6—dc20 96-21723
CIP

Manufactured in the United States of America
10 9 8 7 6 5 4 3 2 1

Series Director: Dominique DeVito
Series Assistant Director: Ariel Cannon
Book Design: Michele Laseau
Cover Design: Iris Jeromnimon
Illustration: Casey Price and Jeff Yesh
Photography:
Front cover: Adult by Paulette Braun/ Pets by Paulette
Puppy by Sian Cox
Back cover: Ellice Hauta
Joan Balzarini: 25, 96
Mary Bloom: 96, 136, 145
Paulette Braun/Pets by Paulette: 2–3, 7, 18, 21, 27, 41, 70, 96
Buckinghamhill American Cocker Spaniels: 148
Sian Cox: 14, 31, 40, 42, 46, 48, 54, 134
Dr. Ian Dunbar: 98, 101, 103, 111, 116–117, 122, 123, 127
Dan Lyons: 96
Cathy Merrithew: 129
Liz Palika: 133
Cheryl Primeau: 23, 68
Susan Rezy: 96–97
Judith Strom: 32, 96, 107, 110, 128, 130, 135, 137, 139, 140, 144, 149, 150
Toni Tucker: 47, 56, 83
Faith Uridel: 5, 11, 13, 52, 61, 62, 63, 65, 67, 72
Zuma Press: 8, 30
Production Team: Kathleen Caulfield, Vic Peterson, Marvin Van Tiem, John Carroll, and Jama Carter

Contents

part one

Welcome to the World of the Chihuahua

part two

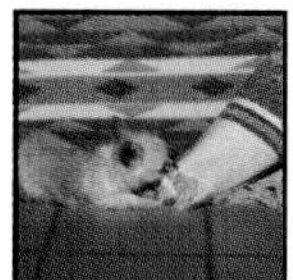

Living with a Chihuahua

part three

Enjoying Your Dog

part four

Beyond the Basics

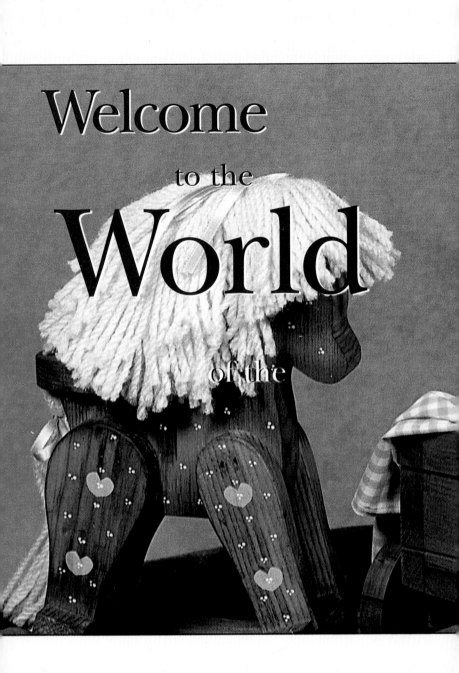

Welcome to the World

of the

part one

Chihuahua

External Features of the Chihuahua 

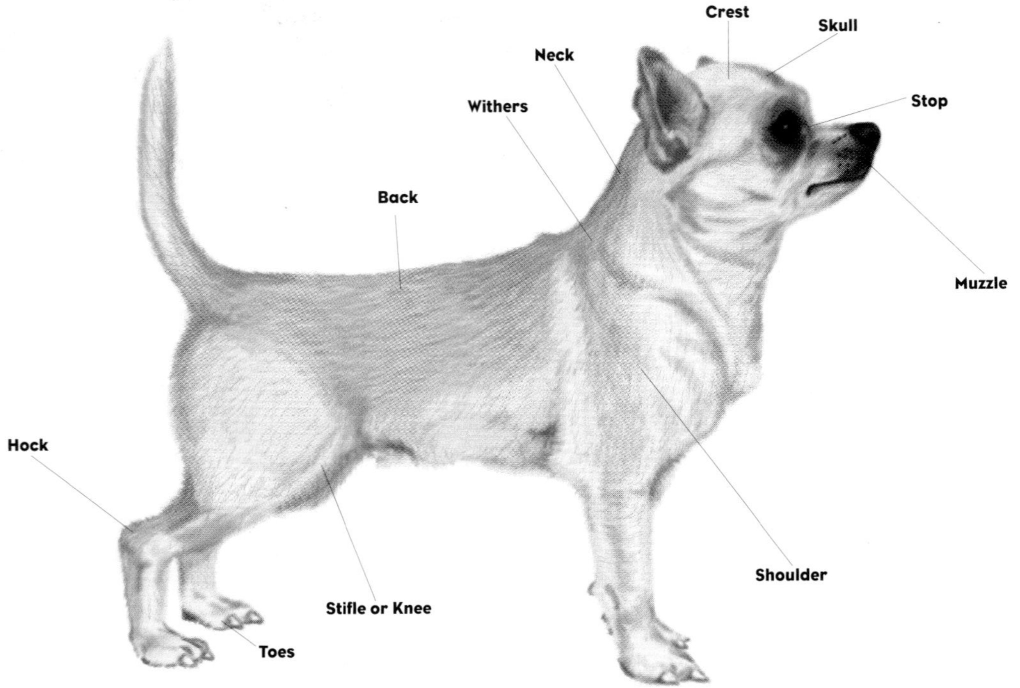

Crest
Skull
Neck
Withers
Stop
Back
Muzzle
Hock
Shoulder
Stifle or Knee
Toes

chapter 1

What Is a Chihuahua?

Chihuahuas, according to the official standard written by the Chihuahua Club of America and approved by the American Kennel Club (AKC), are "graceful, alert, swift-moving, compact, and with a saucy expression." This brief description of the breed is excellent, but it only begins to touch on the essence of the Chihuahua. This chapter will attempt to explicate the appearance and personality of the breed, according to the AKC standard. However, only by owning a Chihuahua will you really know what the breed is like and how it will take you over, body and soul.

The Standard

The standard is a blueprint for a breed that describes the way the dog should look and move. Standards are written by knowledgeable, longtime breeders and are meant to define a breed's type, character, physical description, and usually, its purpose or history. The standard describes the ideal, perfect dog. Of course, there is no "perfect dog," even though every Chihuahua owner thinks his or her dog is perfect! But breeders keep trying to breed as close as possible to their interpretation of the standard. The standard is the guideline breeders use to keep breeding Chihuahuas that look and act like Chihuahuas.

WHAT IS A BREED STANDARD?

A breed standard—a detailed description of an individual breed—is meant to portray the *ideal* specimen of that breed. This includes ideal structure, temperament, gait, type—all aspects of the dog. Because the standard describes an ideal specimen, it isn't based on any particular dog. It is a concept against which judges compare actual dogs and breeders strive to produce dogs. At a dog show, the dog that wins is the one that comes closest, in the judge's opinion, to the standard for its breed. Breed standards are written by the breed parent clubs, the national organizations formed to oversee the well-being of the breed. They are voted on and approved by the members of the parent clubs.

Standards are open to interpretation. Words such as *moderate, slight, narrow, deep,* and *long* are relative and mean different things to different people. Interpreting a standard is subjective, and that is only one of the reasons that different dogs win on different days in show competition.

The standard for the Chihuahua was recorded by the Chihuahua Club of America in 1923. Over the years, there have been changes to the standard, usually for clarification. Even with some slight changes over the years, however, the Chihuahua has remained a relatively stable breed in physical characteristics and has changed very little since its arrival in the United States.

In the following discussion of the standard, the official standard is in italics; the author's commentary follows. For a copy of the complete standard, write the Chihuahua Club of America (*see* address on page 36).

Size

A well-balanced little dog not to exceed 6 pounds.

The Chihuahua has always been known as "the smallest dog in the world!" It was true when the breed first arrived in the United States; it is still true today. Although one will occasionally find tiny specimens of other Toy breeds, this size would not be normal for those breeds; rather these extra small specimens would be considered runts of the litter. The Chihuahua, however, is consistently small, litter after litter, generation after generation.

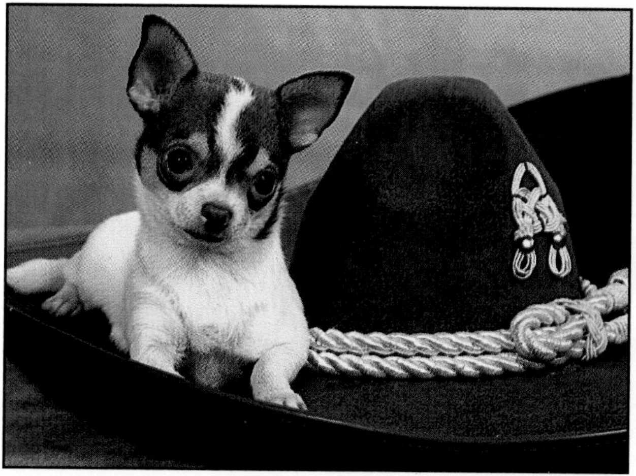

The Chihuahua truly deserves the title "smallest dog in the world."

The Chihuahua is classified as a Toy breed and is shown in the Toy Group at AKC events. Chihuahuas can range in weight up to six pounds. No matter the size within that range, the physical characteristics remain the same.

Head

A well rounded "apple dome" skull, with or without molera. ***Expression****—Saucy.*

Both varieties of the Chihuahua, smooth coat and long coat, have large, well-rounded "apple dome" skulls. The molera is a slight indentation on the top of the skull, like the soft spot on a baby's head. The indentation is not visible but can be felt with a gentle touch.

Although care should be taken not to press on this spot, there should be little concern about this soft area. More details about the molera are in Chapter 7, "Keeping Your Chihuahua Healthy."

Ears

Large, erect type ears, held more upright when alert, but flaring to the sides at a 45 degree angle when in repose, giving breadth between the ears.

Chihuahua ears are quite large and set somewhat low on the head. When the ears are at rest, they point to about ten o'clock and two o'clock. When alert, they are carried closer to eleven o'clock and one o'clock, or slightly higher. Ears that are carried as high as twelve o'clock would be considered too high and would make the dog look rabbitlike.

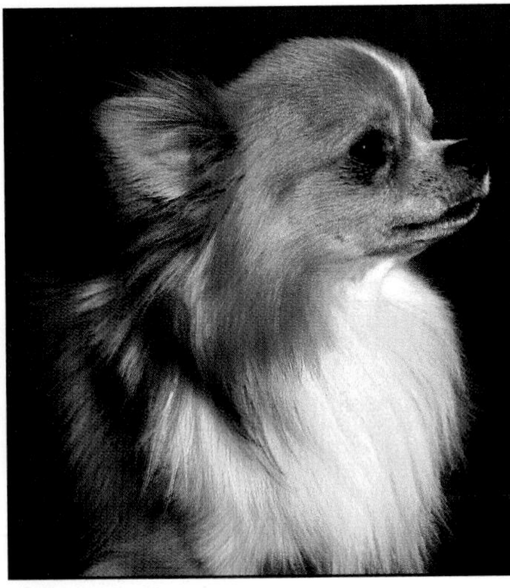

The "apple dome" skull is a hallmark of the breed.

While the puppy is teething, the ears may be up one day and down the next. Ears are usually fully erect between three and six months of age; if the ears are not standing up by eight months of age, they most likely will never become erect. Erect ears or not, you will still have a very nice pet Chihuahua.

Eyes

Full, but not protruding, balanced, well set apart—luminous dark or luminous ruby.

Eyes are somewhat large and full but not protruding. They should never bulge like the eyes of some of the very short-nosed Toy breeds. Although eye color is usually dark, lighter eyes are permissible in light-colored dogs. The ruby eye has a reddish cast to its coloring and is generally found only on very deep red-colored dogs. It is very pretty but is not as common as the dark brown eye.

Bite

Level or scissors.

The bite may be level, with the edges of the upper and lower teeth just touching, or a scissors, with the upper teeth over and slightly covering the top of the bottom teeth, like a pair of scissors.

Muzzle

Moderately short, slightly pointed. Cheeks and jaws lean.

The muzzle, sometimes called the snout, is moderately short and slightly pointed. An excessively short muzzle is not desirable because the teeth may become crowded or breathing problems, including frequent snorting, may occur.

Although the standard does not mention a stop (the indentation located between the eyes separating the top skull from muzzle), the Chihuahua should have a medium stop. This omission will most likely be corrected when the standard is next revised. It would be impossible to have the round, apple-domed skull and moderately short muzzle without at least a medium stop.

Nose

Self-colored in blond types, or black. In moles, blues, and chocolates, they are self-colored. In blonde types, pink nose permissible.

THE AMERICAN KENNEL CLUB

Familiarly referred to as "the AKC," the American Kennel Club is a nonprofit organization devoted to the advancement of purebred dogs. The AKC maintains a registry of recognized breeds and adopts and enforces rules for dog events including shows, obedience trials, field trials, hunting tests, lure coursing, herding, earthdog trials, agility and the Canine Good Citizen program. It is a club of clubs, established in 1884 and composed, today, of over 500 autonomous dog clubs throughout the United States. Each club is represented by a delegate; the delegates make up the legislative body of the AKC, voting on rules and electing directors. The American Kennel Club maintains the Stud Book, the record of every dog ever registered with the AKC, and publishes a variety of materials on purebred dogs, including a monthly magazine, books and numerous educational pamphlets. For more information, contact the AKC at the address listed in Chapter 13, "Resources," and look for the names of their publications in Chapter 12, "Recommended Reading."

The nose is very dark in dark-colored dogs, and lighter in light-colored dogs. Blue dogs will have a blue nose, and chocolates a chocolate or lighter brown nose. A pink nose is permissible in very light-colored dogs, such as white or cream. Less desirable is the nose that has a light streak running down the middle. This coloration is sometimes referred to as a winter nose, and the light streak may disappear during the summer. The streak is sometimes caused by plastic feeding bowls. If your dog has this light streak down his nose, it is not a sign of illness; it is purely cosmetic.

Body

Neck

Slightly arched, gracefully sloping into lean shoulders.

Topline

Level.

Body

Ribs rounded and well sprung (but not too much "barrel shaped").

The Chihuahua neck has a slight arch to it, and the topline is level. Although the ribs are rounded, they should not be fully rounded like a barrel. The body should be off-square in both males and females. Although the male's may be a little shorter than the female's, the male's body should still be off-square. The Chihuahua must not appear to be square in shape when viewed from a profile.

Tail

Moderately long, carried sickle either up or out, or in a loop over the back with just the tip touching the back.

Tails are moderately long and carried in any one of three positions: in a sickle out from the body, in a sickle upright, or in a loop over the back. The tail should never be carried between the legs, which would indicate fright, chilliness, shyness, illness, or even a broken tail.

Feet

A small dainty foot with toes well split up but not spread, pads cushioned.

All Chihuahua colors and color combinations are acceptable.

Feet are small and dainty, neither round nor pointed, but halfway between. The toes are noticeably separated, but should not be wide apart.

Chihuahua Colors

Color

Any color—Solid, marked or splashed.

Chihuahuas come in all colors, including white, fawn, red, black, and sable, to name just a few. They may also be any combination of those colors, as well as various shades from very light to very dark. There is even a blue, and blue coupled with other colors, such as tan or white, but the blue is not as common as those previously mentioned. Breeders in the United States seem to have no preference in color or markings on their Chihuahuas. This is evident at dog shows where you

will see a myriad of colors and markings on the dogs being exhibited.

Coat

In the smooth coats, *the coat should be of soft texture, close and glossy. Coat placed well over body with ruff on neck preferred, and more scanty over head and ears. In* long coats *the coat should be of a soft texture, either flat or slightly curly, with undercoat preferred.*

There are two varieties of Chihuahua: smooth coat and long coat. Except for coat, there is no difference between the two. All breed characteristics are the same for the two varieties.

The Smooth Chihuahua

The smooth coat Chihuahua has a very short and close-to-the-body coat, and may have an undercoat. An undercoat is a layer of fur under the top, or outer, coat. There may be sparser coat (approaching baldness) on the chest, the temples of the head, the ears, and the underbelly if no undercoat is present. The baldness pattern is nothing to be concerned about; it goes with a smooth coat Chihuahua without an undercoat.

The tail of the smooth coat should be covered with furry hair. The smooth coat should also have a slight ruff around the neck, but no fringes or plume like the long coat variety. If the smooth coat Chihuahua does not have an undercoat, she will not have a full ruff around the neck; neither will she have a tail that is heavily coated. In this respect, the standard is somewhat contradictory because it says that for smooth coats "the coat should be of soft texture, close and glossy. (Heavier coats with undercoats permissible.) Coat placed well over body with ruff on neck preferred, and more scanty on head and ears. Hair on tail preferred furry." In fact, an undercoat *must* be present if the preferred ruff on neck and furry tail are present. It is genetically impossible to have a ruff around the neck and a furry tail on a smooth coat without an undercoat. This contradiction may be clarified when the standard is next revised.

The Long Coat Chihuahua

The long coat Chihuahua has a slightly longer body coat, about one to one-and-one-half inches in length, with a definite undercoat. An undercoat is an absolute necessity in the long coat variety. The long coat Chihuahua has fringe, sometimes called feathering, around the edges of the ears; a ruff around the neck; wisps of hair extending along the back of each leg; long hair, called pants, at the buttocks; and long, flowing hair, called a plume, on the tail. These fringes and plume are called furnishings. If the body coat is thick and full, the furnishings are usually more abundant. The standard neither indicates the amount or length of furnishings required nor mentions the length or thickness of the body coat. Aside from the heavier coat, fringes, and tail plume, the long coat Chihuahua should resemble and have the same physical characteristics and conformation as a smooth coat.

There are two varieties of Chihuahua: smooth coat and long coat.

No matter how heavy a coat a smooth coat Chihuahua has, he is not considered a long coat because he will have no furnishings at the edges of the ears or a plume on the tail.

Gait

The Chihuahua should move swiftly with a firm, sturdy action with good reach in front equal to the drive from the rear.

The movement of a Chihuahua is called double tracking. The legs converge slightly toward an imaginary center line on the ground. As the dog moves away from you, you should see only the two hind legs. As the Chihuahua moves toward you, you should see only the two front legs.

The appearance of a Chihuahua is of a little dog who is graceful but alert; the expression is saucy and full of life. She is a fast-moving little dog who can keep up with you as you walk along. She should appear to be happy and full of vitality as she trots by your side, with her head and tail up.

Temperament

Alert, with terrier-like qualities.

The Chihuahua is an alert little dog with a saucy expression.

The temperament of the Chihuahua is primarily based on two important factors: inherited traits and proper socialization. For any breed of dog, particularly for dogs as small as the Chihuahua, early socialization outside the family circle is of the utmost importance. If a Chihuahua is kept within the confines of his usual human family and rarely interacts with other people, it is highly unlikely that this size dog will retain her natural friendly disposition. A puppy must be descended from friendly tempered parents and must receive socialization outside her immediate family at a young age, preferably before eight weeks. If these conditions are met, the puppy should grow up to be friendly and happy with everyone, family and welcomed strangers.

In any event, once you have owned a Chihuahua, you will most likely be a fan of the breed for life.

chapter 2

The Chihuahua's Ancestry

It is said that all dog breeds evolved from only one wild ancestor. Contemporary dog breeds were created and domesticated through selective breeding. People bred for the qualities they desired for certain useful purposes. That's why we have breeds that can track, herd, hunt, guard, and go to ground. And that's why there are breeds that are strictly companion animals. The Chihuahua is generally classified in the companion dog division primarily because of its diminutive size, even though it can be trained to do many useful things.

Ch. Hurd's LIL Indian (1968)

The Chihuahua's ancestry is so steeped in myth, secondhand stories, and controversial history that it is almost impossible to separate fact

from fiction. The little that was recorded in bygone days was written in archaic Spanish, making later interpretation difficult. Several theories of the Chihuahua's origin are presented here because all the fables, legends and stories are fun to read and discuss, even though they may not be true.

This clay figure is thought by some to be a depiction of the Chihuahua's ancestors.

Mexican Origins

There are those who insist that the Chihuahua is a native Mexican breed because ancient relics of small doglike creatures were found in the archeological remains of the Mayans, the Toltecs and the Aztecs.

The National Museum in Mexico City houses some interesting sculptures; one is of a small dog with large ears, kissing its master. Another sculpture depicts a woman and child; the woman is carrying a small, erect-eared dog, supposedly a Chihuahua, under one arm.

However, Mayan history is very obscure, and some of these early statues bear little or no resemblance to the modern-day Chihuahua.

Chihuahuas in Toltec Civilization

Sketchy information is available about the Toltec culture, which existed around the ninth century in what is now Mexico. Many believe that the modern-day Chihuahua is a direct descendant of a dog called the Techichi, depicted in the stone carvings of the monastery of Huejotzingo. The small dogs pictured there bear a more striking resemblance to our present-day Chihuahua.

According to a theory that first appeared in print in 1904, the Techichi was crossed with a wild breed called the Perro Chihuahueno. This breed originally lived in the wild mountains of Chihuahua, where it foraged on anything edible. The dogs supposedly lived in holes in the ground; possessed round heads, short pointed noses, large erect ears, slender legs, and long toenails; and were wild and untrainable.

Chihuahuas in Aztec Culture

The statues from the Aztec era bear an even more striking resemblance to our current dogs. The Aztecs were the conquerors of the Toltecs, and their civilization flourished for several centuries. A small dog was particularly revered by the Aztecs and became the prized possession of the rich. It is said that these little dogs were so treasured by royalty that some families had as many as several hundred specimens. The little dogs supposedly led a life of luxury and were pampered and cared for by slaves; they were even fed a special diet. During that period, the blue Chihuahua was considered especially sacred. Even today, a blue Chihuahua is unusual.

The little dogs were even buried with their wealthy owners because it was believed that the sins of the interred would be transmitted to the dog, thus ensuring a safe resting

Where Did Dogs Come From?

It can be argued that dogs were right there at man's side from the beginning of time. As soon as human beings began to document their own existence, the dog was among their drawings and inscriptions. Dogs were not just friends, they served a purpose: There were dogs to hunt birds, pull sleds, herd sheep, burrow after rats—even sit in laps! What your dog was originally bred to do influences the way it behaves. The American Kennel Club recognizes over 140 breeds, and there are hundreds more distinct breeds around the world. To make sense of the breeds, they are grouped according to their size or function. The AKC has seven groups:

1) Sporting, 2) Working,
3) Herding, 4) Hounds,
5) Terriers, 6) Toys,
7) Non-Sporting

Can you name a breed from each group? Here's some help: (1) Golden Retriever; (2) Doberman Pinscher; (3) Collie; (4) Beagle; (5) Scottish Terrier; (6) Maltese; and (7) Dalmatian. All modern domestic dogs (*Canis familiaris*) are related, however different they look, and are all descended from *Canis lupus*, the gray wolf.

place for the master. It was also believed that the little dog would see his master safely along the journey through the underworld, guiding the deceased through all kinds of dangerous places in the afterlife.

Mediterranean Roots

Some people believe that the Chihuahua originated in some Mediterranean countries and then became established on the island of Malta. A small dog with the molera trait, common only to the Chihuahua, inhabited that island. From there, the breed was supposed to have been introduced to European countries via trading ships.

The Chihuahua is generally considered to be of Mexican origin.

Small dogs resembling Chihuahuas can be found in many paintings by European masters. The most noted work is a fresco created by Sondro Botticelli, circa 1482, located in the Sistine Chapel. The painting is one of a series depicting the life of Moses and clearly shows a small, round-headed, smooth-coated little dog with long nails, large eyes, and large ears that closely resembles a modern-day Chihuahua. Because this painting was created before Columbus arrived in the New World, it leads one to reconsider the theory that the Chihuahua is a truly Mexican dog.

Because of the evidence in these early European paintings, others believe that the Chihuahua was introduced to Mexico by the Spanish invaders. However, from the time of the Spanish conquest to the mid-1800s, little is known of the Chihuahua. The Aztec's magnificent civilization was destroyed by the Spanish invaders, along with all information pertaining to the Chihuahua.

With all these theories, you can pick and choose what to believe about the origin of the Chihuahua.

The Chihuahua Comes to the United States

Although it is true that Chihuahua-like remains have been found in some parts of Mexico, I surmise that the reason many people believe the Chihuahua to be of Mexican origin is because it was along the border of Mexico and the United States that the breed became more popular and sought after from the mid-1800s onward. Americans became very interested in the breed around the 1850s.

Ch. Dartan's Blazon Dragon (1969) has the distinct ears, large eyes, and rounded skull that first captivated Chihuahua admirers.

When the breed was first introduced to the United States, the dogs were not called Chihuahuas. They were usually referred to as Arizona Dogs or Texas Dogs because they were often found along the U.S.-Mexican border. Later, many American tourists, fascinated by these tiny specimens, purchased the dogs from residents of Mexico, and the dogs became known as Mexican Chihuahuas. Chihuahua is the largest northern state of Mexico, where many remains of small dogs resembling the breed were found. Today, the word *Mexican* has been dropped and the breed is simply called the Chihuahua. In Mexico, the breed is called Chihuahueno.

One of the earliest published articles pertaining to the Chihuahua was written in 1914 by James Watson, an early importer of the breed. In 1888, Watson bought his first Chihuahua for three dollars from a Mexican.

The Chihuahua was extremely tiny and did not survive for more than a year. Sometime later, Watson was able to buy several other Chihuahuas from Arizona, Texas, and Mexico. He spoke of the Chihuahua as being smart, bright, and very affectionate. Watson maintained that unless the dog had a molera in the middle of the top skull, it was not purebred. Basically, the Chihuahuas he describes in his writings are recognizable as the Chihuahuas of today.

The long coat Chihuahua is not a new variety. In fact, some of the first Chihuahuas brought into the United States were long coats.

Show Ring History

In 1884, the first Chihuahua to be exhibited at an American dog show was classified as a Chihuahua-Terrier and was shown in the Miscellaneous Class. This class was for foreign and unclassified breeds.

One hundred years later, at a show in Philadelphia in November 1984, twenty-six smooth coat Chihuahuas and twenty-five long coat Chihuahuas were in the regular breed classes and five Chihuahuas competed in the obedience trial.

Chihuahua Popularity

The first Chihuahua registered with the AKC was named Midget. He was born July 18, 1903, and owned by H. Raynor of El Paso, Texas. There were five registrations of Chihuahuas that year, four in the name of

H. Raynor and one registered in the name of J. M. Lee of Los Angeles, also bred by Mr. Raynor.

In 1904, just eleven Chihuahuas were exhibited, but twelve years later, in 1916, fifty Chihuahuas were exhibited at AKC events. By 1967, the popularity of the Chihuahua was increasing rapidly, and that year more than 37,000 Chihuahuas were registered with the AKC. The breed waned in popularity during the 1970s but is once again on the rise. During the 1990s it is in the top twenty most popular breeds registered with the AKC.

Famous Chihuahuas

As early as the latter part of the 1800s, Chihuahuas broke into show business. A British performer, Rosina Casselli, had a group of at least a dozen Chihuahuas in her stage act performing all kinds of tricks.

It's easy to see why the Chihuahua is one of the most popular breeds.

Many people were familiar with the sight of the late Xavier Cugat, noted Latin American bandleader, carrying his Chihuahua with him on stage at each performance. There was even a tale about Mr. Cugat's smuggling his Chihuahua into his hotel room (no dogs were allowed in hotel rooms at that time) by disguising the dog as a baby, complete with bonnet!

General Santa Ana, former president of Mexico, was an enthusiastic Chihuahua owner. Unfortunately, during one of his wartime excursions, his dogs disappeared. To this day, no one has been able to account for the missing Chihuahuas.

FAMOUS OWNERS OF CHIHUAHUAS

Billie Holiday

Martina Navratilova

Mickey Rourke

Rosie O'Donnell

Arnold Schwarzenegger

Gertrude Stein

Vincent Price

Charo

Herman Hickman, a huge man and former Yale football coach, owned two tiny three-pound Chihuahuas named Slugger and Killer.

The fantastic jazz singer, the late Billie Holiday, was a devoted Chihuahua owner, as was the noted singer-actress-comedienne of the 1980s, Christine Ebersole.

Chihuahuas have been depicted in Disney films, television shows, Broadway plays, cartoons, print ads, photographic exhibits, art shows and television series. They have been performers on many late-night talk shows. The author's dogs have appeared on television many times, including network and PBS shows, and have modeled for many print advertisements. Chihuahuas make wonderful models because they are easily trained and respond well to direction.

Chihuahuas in Art

Many famous artists depicted Chihuahuas in their paintings. The National Gallery of Art in Washington, D.C., has a Henri de Toulouse-Lautrec painting entitled "Lady with a Dog"; this painting shows a tiny, smooth-coated Chihuahua-type dog.

Many beautiful paintings can be seen at the headquarters of the AKC in New York City or at the Dog Museum in St. Louis.

chapter 3

The World According to the Chihuahua

The Chihuahua has been consistently popular since its arrival in the United States. Why are these little dogs so beloved? The answers are numerous. Besides being cute, cuddly, charming, affectionate, and bright, they are easy to manage and to take with you everywhere; they are not costly to maintain; they are outgoing; they are great watchdogs; they are healthy, loyal and devoted to their owners; they do not roam away from home; they require little space and little exercise.

Who Should Own a Chihuahua?

The Chihuahua is ideal for older people who cannot manage larger, stronger dogs and for persons and families in small living quarters.

Chihuahuas make wonderful companions and can go almost anywhere, even under your seat on an airplane.

Chihuahuas are not for everyone. They are not for people who are rough—adults or children. The Chihuahua is not for you if you are worried about your furniture and rugs or if you imagine doggy odor even when there isn't any. If you worry about what mischief your puppy will get into (and a puppy will get into all kinds of mischief), you are probably not a candidate for ownership of any breed!

A DOG'S SENSES

Sight: With their eyes located farther apart than ours, dogs can detect movement at a greater distance than we can, but they can't see as well up close. They can also see better in less light, but can't distinguish many colors.

Sound: Dogs can hear about four times better than we can, and they can hear high-pitched sounds especially well. Their ancestors, the wolves, howled to let other wolves know where they were; our dogs do the same, but they have a wider range of vocalizations, including barks, whimpers, moans and whines.

Smell: A dog's nose is his greatest sensory organ. His sense of smell is so great he can follow a trail that's weeks old, detect odors diluted to one-millionth the concentration we'd need to notice them, even sniff out a person under water!

Taste: Dogs have fewer taste buds than we do, so they're likelier to try anything—and usually do, which is why it's especially important for their owners to monitor their food intake. Dogs are omnivores, which means they eat meat as well as vegetable matter like grasses and weeds.

Touch: Dogs are social animals and love to be petted, groomed and played with.

Some people think that a Chihuahua is not a "man's dog," but often, the "man of the house" is completely won over by a little three- or four-pound Chihuahua! He might tell you that a Chihuahua is not a real dog or that dogs should be large and useful, but sooner or later, and more likely sooner, he will succumb to the charms of this breed.

Chihuahuas and Children

Chihuahuas are probably not the breed to keep with a small child. A young child might accidentally fall on the dog, causing serious injury or even death to the Chihuahua. A child may think of the Chihuahua as another squeezable plaything, but a hard squeeze could seriously injure a Chihuahua. Dogs of this size should not be left with children unattended, for both the child's and the dog's sake.

Children can make a dog feel threatened. When the dog gives a warning growl, many children ignore the noise, not realizing the dog is serious. But any dog can take only so much teasing and will most likely strike back by biting the child. Children must be taught how to interact safely and humanely with dogs, particularly small ones. On the other hand, children who know how to treat a small dog like the Chihuahua properly can be wonderful companions.

Lap Dogs

Chihuahuas might be classified as "lap dogs and cuddlers." They enjoy being with you all the time, whether they are awake or sleeping. They love to travel with you. For every affectionate pat they receive, you will get double payback in love and loyalty.

Chihuahuas are affectionate and loyal to their people. These two are sharing a smile.

Chihuahuas like to be massaged and will often roll over for a belly rub. Use caution when massaging a puppy's ears to avoid damaging the ear cartilage, which would prevent the ears from becoming erect.

The Chihuahua is happiest when he is around people, particularly his owner. He likes to cuddle, sit in your lap, be by your side, and sleep in your bed. However, though you may like to be by your Chihuahua at all times, it is not safe to have him in your bed at night. You may accidentally roll on top of the dog in the middle of the night. I recommend that you train your dog to sleep in his own bed or in a crate. This is purely a safety measure for the Chihuahua.

Chihuahuas are Long-Lived

Chihuahuas live a very long time, twenty-plus years in some cases. Provide your Chihuahua with the proper medical care, a loving environment, and responsible training, and you will enjoy a long and rewarding relationship with him. Of all the breeds registered with the AKC, the Chihuahua is one of the most affectionate, popular and long-lived breeds.

Chihuahuas are Low-Maintenance

Grooming Needs

The Chihuahua is considered a natural dog; there is no docking of tails and no cropping of ears. The coat is not trimmed, stripped, shaved or plucked. The dog is extremely easy to care for and maintain.

Exercise Needs

Compared to a dog of fifty-plus pounds, a Chihuahua does not need a great deal of exercise. Much of this exercise is provided by just running around the house. Additional exercise can be achieved by providing the dog with a partially shaded run, which will give the dog a place where she can trot back and forth.

Playtime with your Chihuahua can be a form of exercise for both of you. A Chihuahua will chase a ball, catch a soft disc, and retrieve small items. Whatever you use for playtime, be certain that the item is not so small that the Chihuahua could swallow it. Do not give your dog toys with eyes that could fall out, toys with strings or ribbons, or toys with internal noisemakers that could be torn out and swallowed. If the toy can fit easily into the Chihuahua's mouth, it is too small and dangerous for the dog to play with.

If jogging is your thing, do not overdo this exercise with your Chihuahua. A two-mile run may be okay for you, but not for your Chihuahua. A young Chihuahua will have a very short endurance, perhaps only a few yards. An older Chihuahua would be able to trot with you over a greater distance, but certainly not more than half a mile. Remember that a human stride of three feet is quite a distance for a tiny dog.

Chihuahuas like to accompany their owners for short walks, but be prepared to have the walk constantly interrupted by strangers who will inquire about these tiny, saucy, pert and inquisitive little bundles of fur. If the dog gets tired while on a walk with you, carry him before he gets physically exhausted.

Adaptable to All Spaces

Chihuahuas make good pets and companions in most climates and living quarters. They adapt well to most homes, whether houses, apartments or condos. (If you live in an apartment or condo, be certain that pets are allowed, especially because the Chihuahua's bark is loud and shrill.)

Chihuahuas are ideal dogs for many people because they can fit almost anywhere.

Chihuahuas with Other Dogs

Chihuahuas usually get along well with other dog breeds, but when a small dog is first introduced into the household of another dog of any breed, they must be supervised until the owner is certain that the various sizes are getting along well together.

Shedding

Both long coat and smooth coat Chihuahuas will shed their coats from time to time, but shedding can be kept at a minimum by appropriate grooming techniques. (*See* Chapter 6, "How to Groom Your Chihuahua.")

Snorting and Snoring

The Chihuahua usually does not snore, but occasionally, one will do so. Snoring may be due to a muzzle that is too short, in which case there is no remedy for the condition. Occasionally, a Chihuahua will snort, which is sometimes referred to as a reverse sneeze. A snort occurs because the dog is so close to the ground that dust gets into the nostrils. To alleviate this condition, make a cup with the palm of your hand and place it gently over your dog's nose without cutting off his oxygen. Breathing in this pocket of warm air will usually stop the snorting. Repeat two or three times as necessary.

Chihuahuas Make Good Watchdogs

Chihuahuas do not bark any more than other breeds of dogs, and they can be gently trained to be quiet on command, but they should be allowed to bark at the approach of strangers and at unusual situations for your protection. You should discourage excessive and constant barking for no reason.

Chihuahuas are excellent watchdogs. Their hearing is acute, and their bark is loud and shrill. Chihuahuas have been known to scare burglars and warn owners of fire and other dangers. Because the dog's hearing is so sharp, a Chihuahua will alert the family before anyone in the household is aware of impending disaster. One owner claims that his Chihuahua has always warned him of snakes in his backyard! Another Chihuahua alerted his owner to an intruder entering the house in the middle of the night. The burglar did not stay long; he was deterred by the loud and constant barking.

Chihuahuas will not run up to a visiting houseguest and jump all over the person. They are cautious about accepting a stranger at face value and may continue to bark until ordered to be quiet. Your Chihuahua will not be aggressive but will look over the guest from a distance, approaching with caution before deciding all is well. The guest should allow the Chihuahua to take the initiative and make the first friendly overtures; this will put the dog more at ease. This does not mean your dog is shy—just aware that a nonfamily member is in the house.

CHARACTERISTICS OF THE CHIHUAHUA

affectionate

long-lived

delicate

requires minimal grooming and exercise

has a shrill, loud bark

needs to be kept warm

With a dog as small as a Chihuahua, the guest should not bend over the dog when he or she approaches because the dog may interpret this as a menacing move. Instead, the person should try squatting to caress the dog. The next step is to try petting the Chihuahua's chest, neck, shoulder or back, which is less menacing than reaching for the top of the head.

This cautious awareness of surroundings and people may be due to the Chihuahua's diminutiveness. If the dog were to eagerly run up to a guest, the person could scoop up the dog quickly, perhaps dropping or injuring him in some manner. If a Chihuahua eagerly accepted strangers, he would not be much of a watchdog. Chihuahuas do not like people, especially strangers, rushing and grabbing at them.

Socializing Your Chihuahua

If you do not want your Chihuahua to become aggressive, play gently with him. Otherwise, he will think that aggressive behavior is tolerated, and you'll never know when it might erupt. If the Chihuahua was taught to play in an aggressive manner or to attack, he could bite his next playmate, be it another dog or a human being.

Chihuahuas Need to Be Kept Warm

The Chihuahua likes to lie directly in the sun shining through the window. He also likes to be near the heater in the winter, though this can dry out the coat. (*See* Chapter 6, "Feeding Your Chihuahua," for information on preventing the coat from drying out.) The Chihuahua particularly likes to be in his own snuggly bed when the air is too cool. One of the ways your Chihuahua will keep warm is to curl up into a round ball and tuck his nose under a leg. This will give the dog a pocket of warm air to inhale that, in turn, will help keep him warm.

Chihuahuas will keep warm by tucking themselves into a snug ball.

Some Chihuahuas shiver and shake, which can usually be attributed to fright or a chill. If it is fright from loud noises, unfamiliar surroundings, or previous abusive treatment, obedience classes may help overcome the shaking by building up the dog's confidence.

Chihuahuas get cold easily, so shaking is likely from a chill. If you live where the winters are cold, a sweater will be necessary for your Chihuahua if you will be outside for more than five minutes. A word of caution is in order for winter walks. Salt, sand, and ice melters are outdoor winter hazards that will play havoc with your dog's feet, so be sure to wipe and clean the Chihuahua's feet after a winter walk. A dog can get frostbite, even lose toes, so be well aware of this when outside for any length of time.

Owning More Than One Chihuahua

It is not unusual for many Chihuahua owners to have not one, but two Chihuahuas as family members. Two dogs mean more care and training but, in general, double the enjoyment for the family. Also, the two Chihuahuas will provide company and play companions for each other in a sort of buddy system. One of the two, however, will become "top dog" and may very well boss the other Chihuahua around. If two or more Chihuahuas are in residence, each will develop its own distinct personality. With more than one Chihuahua in the same household, it is recommended that they be the same sex or that they both be spayed or neutered. Then it will not matter.

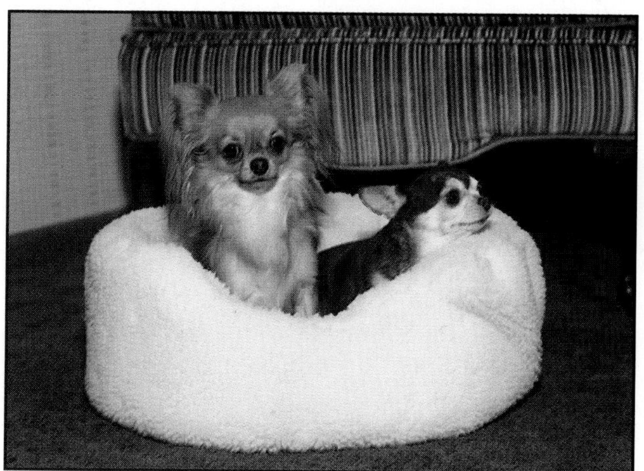

Two Chihuahuas will be companions and playmates for each other.

Chihuahua Activities

Obedience Instruction

Even little dogs like the Chihuahua can become pests if not properly trained, so some basic obedience training is recommended. It is important that this training be gentle, positive and firm. Young puppies have a short attention span and are easily distracted.

I recommend observing an obedience class and instructor before enrolling the dog in that class. Try to find a training course conducted by an instructor who has had experience with tiny dogs. Consult other people who have attended obedience classes; perhaps your veterinarian can help you in selecting a class. Consult the local kennel club, the regional Chihuahua club, or the local dog obedience club. The location of these clubs and other pertinent information can be obtained from the AKC (*see* page 36 for address). There are all sorts of activities you and your Chihuahua can compete or participate in.

With positive, gentle training, the Chihuahua will excel in competition, like this one in Open Agility.

Hearing Ear Dog

Chihuahuas' small size, intelligence and excellent hearing make them perfect candidates for this line of work. Often, smaller dogs are preferred in the apartments or condos of older beneficiaries. Hearing ear dogs are responsible for alerting their owners to common household noises, such as the doorbell, telephone, tea kettle or smoke alarm. They have obedience training as well as specialized hearing ear training, and their owners usually communicate with them through a system of hand signals. The presence of a hearing ear dog often makes a huge difference in the lives of people with hearing impairments.

Therapy Dog

The role of therapy dogs has grown significantly in the last ten years. Now, dogs are commonly brought as visitors to nursing homes and other institutions in which the residents are not allowed to keep their own pets. The presence of these pets is often the brightest moment of the day. A well-behaved Chihuahua has much to contribute on these occasions. Their friendly nature and small size make them perfect candidates for lap visits.

To get involved with a pet therapy organization in your area, contact the Delta Society (289 Perimeter Rd. East, Renton, WA 98055-1329 or call 206-226-7357), or your local kennel club.

Traveling with Your Chihuahua

If you are considering bringing your Chihuahua on a trip with you, first make sure he will be welcome. If you are visiting friends or relatives, make sure they like your dog and know how to treat him properly, and that they don't have pets or children who won't get along with him. If you are planning to stay in a hotel or motel, make sure beforehand that dogs are welcome. Many places that welcome animals have restrictions on the time of year and the number of dogs staying at one time. Plan well in advance and don't be surprised when you arrive!

Traveling by Car

Contain your Chihuahua in his crate while the car is in motion. This is much safer for both the dog and the human passengers; you don't want to run the risk he will startle the driver or get trapped under the driver's feet. Secure the crate in the back seat with the seatbelt or with bungee cords. Make sure the crate is secure so it does not lurch forward if you have to brake suddenly.

Bring along food and drinking water, cozy blankets and some favorite toys. Take a break every few hours to let your Chihuahua out to stretch and relieve himself.

Traveling by Plane

If your pet will travel with you by air, an airline crate is a must. An airline crate must be sturdy and the bottom solid. The mesh should be fine enough so that a foot or tail cannot slip out. You can arrange for the dog to be shipped as cargo, in which case he will be kept in a pressurized compartment with a temperature about

the same as the passenger cabin. Some airlines will allow small dogs to be in the cabin with the owner if they are contained in a crate placed under the seat. The airline must approve this in advance, and the carrier must be no larger than any other carry-on luggage. With a tiny Chihuahua, this should not present a problem. Your Chihuahua will tolerate this confinement as long as he is close to you and you can reassure him.

When Your Chihuahua Can't Come with You

In many cases it is much wiser to leave your dog behind than to take him with you when you travel. It is unkind to leave your dog in a strange environment for long periods while you sightsee or visit with family. Take some time to organize the best possible accommodations for your dog beforehand so you can enjoy your trip without worrying how your Chihuahua is faring.

Whenever you leave your Chihuahua, do your part to ensure his comfort before you leave. See if you can get a friend or relative to play with him or walk him a few times a week. If your Chihuahua will be boarding at the kennel, take along a few favorite toys. Leave detailed instructions with whomever will be caring for your Chihuahua. In case of emergency, make sure to provide your vet's telephone number and a number at which you can be reached.

Kennel Accommodations

Don't just send your dog to the first place listed in the Yellow Pages. Get referrals from your vet, breeder and other pet owners in your area. Visit the kennel before you drop off your Chihuahua, and look for clean facilities, both an indoor and outdoor run for the animals, and a genuinely attentive staff. Make sure the kennel requires proof of shots, including one for kennel cough. There should be an attendant on the premises twenty four hours a day.

In-Home Pet Care

With this method of pet care, your Chihuahua will be able to remain in his home, and will not be exposed to fleas or germs from other dogs, as he would in a kennel environment. However, there are drawbacks as well. Your Chihuahua may be lonely and unhappy, and may take to chewing things or being otherwise destructive in your absence. Also, do you mind giving a stranger access to your home while you are away? Again, ask a trusted authority for recommendations about in-home care personnel. Meet with the person beforehand and introduce him or her to the dog. Don't settle for someone you aren't comfortable with.

More Information About Chihuahuas

The National Breed Club

The Chihuahua Club of America, Inc.
5019 Village Trail
San Antonio, TX 78218

The club can send you information on all aspects of the breed including the names and addresses of breed clubs in your area, as well as obedience clubs. Inquire about membership.

Specialists in Small Dog Obedience Equipment

J & J Dog Supplies
P.O. Box 1517
Galesburg, IL 61402

Max 200
14 Morris Avenue
Mountain Lakes, NJ 07046

Paul's Obedience Shop
P.O. Box 767
Hanover, PA 17331-0767

Sylvia's Tack Box
4333 11th Street A
Moline, IL 61265

Books

Terry, E. Ruth. *The New Chihuahua.* New York: Howell Book House, 1990.

Nicholas, Anna Katherine. *The Chihuahua.* Neptune, New Jersey: T.F.H. Publications, 1988.

Pisano, Beverly. *Chihuahuas.* Neptune, New Jersey: T.F.H. Publications, 1988.

Cecil, Barbara and Gerianne Darnell. *Competitive Obedience Training For The Small Dog.* Council Bluffs, Iowa: T9E Publishing.

Tellington-Jones, Linda. *The Tellington Touch.* Santa Fe, New Mexico: self-published.

Please contact the author at the address or phone number below for information about the availability of the book. It is also available on videotape.

P.O.Box 3793
Santa Fe, NM 87501
1-800-854-TEAM

Magazines

Los Chihuahuas
12860 Thonotosassa Road
Dover, FL 33527

Videos

The American Kennel Club. *The Chihuahua.*

See Chapter 13, "Resources," for a complete listing of dog-related organizations.

Living
with a

part two

Chihuahua

chapter 4

Bringing Your Chihuahua Home

Raising and training a puppy of any breed is a huge responsibility. When you begin to think about getting a puppy, make sure you are ready for this kind of commitment. Ask yourself the following: Do I really want a Chihuahua? Can I afford to maintain a dog? Will a Chihuahua fit my lifestyle? Am I responsible enough to care for the dog for his entire life? If you can answer these questions with an unqualified "yes," then the next question is: Where do I get my Chihuahua puppy?

Choosing Your Chihuahua Puppy

Your local kennel club is a good place to start. These all-breed organizations usually keep a list of reputable breeders in your area. Other resources to try include the AKC, which can furnish the name and address of the local Chihuahua club as well as the Chihuahua Club of America. Pet stores or your veterinarian may have a similar list of breeders in your area.

Chihuahua litters are very small, averaging one to three puppies per litter, so it may be a little difficult to find a puppy. Have no fear, however, Chihuahua breeders are always in touch with one another, even cross-country, so someone will know where to find puppies. You may have to travel a little to see the puppies, but the trip will be worth it because you will be able to see the puppies in their home environment.

If you have the opportunity to go to the breeder's home, you will also have a chance to see the mother, and perhaps the father (or a picture of him) and grandparents as well. Observe these relatives; their appearance and behavior will give you a good idea of the kind of dog your puppy will be at maturity.

Chihuahua puppies are irresistible, but they require commitment, love and care.

Take your family with you when choosing a puppy. It is important that everyone agrees on the puppy selection. Remember that dog ownership is a lifetime family responsibility!

Wherever you find your puppy, try to visit more than once before buying. Get a true feel for the puppy you will be choosing; you do not want to get home wishing that you had made another puppy selection. Look for a healthy, outgoing puppy who is eager to interact with people and things in her environment. Do not pick a puppy because you feel sorry for him. A shy puppy may grow into a timid, fearful, and ill-tempered adult. Be certain the puppy does not show signs of illness, such as lethargy, eye discharge (do not confuse this with tear staining, common in Chihuahuas because of small tear ducts), missing patches of coat,

or unsteady gait. The puppy should be free of external and internal parasites, though the latter must be determined by a veterinarian.

Be prepared to be questioned by the breeder from whom you are buying the Chihuahua. A truly responsible breeder will want to know if the puppy is going to a family in which the dog will have a caring home for its entire life. The breeder will also observe and ask questions of you and your family while you are selecting a puppy. These measures are taken to ensure the puppy's safety and are good indicators of responsible breeding and caring dog ownership.

You may consider the initial cost of a Chihuahua puppy to be high, but if the cost is divided over the life span of the dog, it is minimal. Remember that you are not buying a dog by the pound. The cost of love and companionship received can not be equated with money.

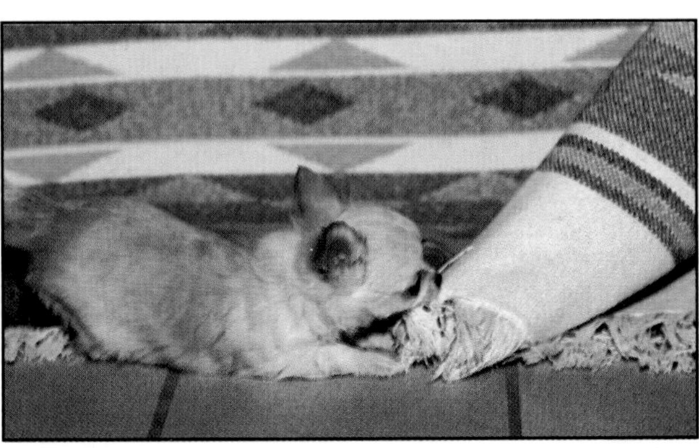

Curious puppies will play with and put just about anything in their mouths.

Preparing for Your New Puppy

Before your new puppy arrives, be sure to have his new home ready. Provide a bed with a washable pillow and blanket; a crate with pillow and blanket, toys for play and chewing, and baby gates if you want to close off parts of the house, particularly carpeted areas.

Puppy Proofing

Make certain that your Chihuahua's sleeping and play areas are puppy proof. There should be nothing that the puppy can get into that will injure or poison him. Get rid of any sharp or very small objects that puppy could swallow. Do not leave plastic bags around; a puppy could suffocate in these. Remove electrical cords the puppy could chew on. Plants must be out of reach.

Keep all medications, house-cleaning materials, soaps, sponges, paints, disinfectants, health aids, makeup, hair preparations, aspirin, laxatives, ointments, perfumes, and shampoos in tightly covered containers or in cupboards with latches that lock.

Outside, close garbage lids tightly. Scrub away any antifreeze, brake fluid, gasoline, or windshield washer fluid that has settled on the driveway or garage floor. Tightly close all pest control products and place them on a high shelf in the garage. Always think of your puppy as a curious baby, ready to get into anything and everything, and take the proper precautions to eliminate all potential dangers. Adult Chihuahuas do not seem to get in as much trouble with these things, but do not take any chances.

Because puppies will attempt to eat anything, be very careful about what is available to your Chihuahua. Dogs have been known to eat nails, Ping Pong balls and stones. Dog owners must be alert at all times, especially with a young, curious puppy.

Supplies

Grooming Equipment

Grooming tools, such as a comb, brush and nail clippers will soon be needed. Grooming equipment is discussed in detail in Chapter 6, "Grooming Your Chihuahua."

Yard Preparation

A small fenced-in area in your backyard will provide puppy a play area as well as a place to relieve himself. The fenced-in area should be partially shaded from the sun and other weather elements. Clean water should always be available. The run need not be large and should always be kept clean and free of feces.

Chihuahuas are house dogs and must not be left out for long periods in any kind of weather. Chihuahua puppies have been known to squeeze through a chain-link fence or between the small openings where the gate attaches to a panel of links. Get a fence in which the links are close together, and be certain there is little, if any, space where partitions come together.

Food and Water Dishes

Use small food dishes and water dishes that do not tip over easily. Stainless-steel dishes are best for your Chihuahua. There are also bowls that can be hooked on the side of the Chihuahua's crate.

Toys

Provide your Chihuahua puppy with plenty of safe toys to keep him active and stimulated. Make sure toys do not have small parts that can be bitten off; if stuffing comes out of stuffed toys, remove them immediately. Cloth toys should be washable. Pieces of string or ribbon from packages are not suitable playthings for your Chihuahua.

Do not give your Chihuahua old shoes or socks to play with. He will not know the difference between old and new shoes, and it could encourage bad behavior. You would not want to arrive home to find your best shoes torn to shreds. The same holds true for any personal item of clothing or other personal belongings.

Suitable toys include nylon bones, which are great for chewing and gnawing. They will keep your Chihuahua entertained and keep his teeth free of tartar. Another good toy for healthy teeth is a rope toy, made of thick rope tied at each end. Toys that encourage you to interact with your dog are also a great idea. Balls and toys of all kinds can turn into retrievable items you and your pet can enjoy together.

Your Puppy's Crate

There are various types of crates available. The hard or soft plastic ones should be used only in the winter. They are much too hot for summer travel, and your

Chihuahua would not get enough cool ventilated air. For warm weather, use a wire crate, also known as an open crate. If you wish to use a wire crate year-round, there are insulated covers that fit nicely over the wire crates, and these covers help keep your Chihuahua warm during inclement weather. If using a cover, make certain there is a "window" for your Chihuahua to look through and an open area for ventilation.

Feed your puppy in the crate, and he will associate the crate with pleasantness rather than punishment. Crates and collars will quickly become a pleasant experience with this method.

> **HOUSEHOLD DANGERS**
>
> Curious puppies and inquisitive dogs get into trouble not because they are bad, but simply because they want to investigate the world around them. It's our job to protect our dogs from harmful substances, like the following:
>
> **IN THE HOUSE**
>
> cleaners, especially pine oil
>
> perfumes, colognes, aftershaves
>
> medications, vitamins
>
> office and craft supplies
>
> electric cords
>
> chicken or turkey bones
>
> chocolate
>
> some house and garden plants, like ivy, oleander and poinsettia
>
> **IN THE GARAGE**
>
> antifreeze
>
> garden supplies, like snail and slug bait, pesticides, fertilizers, mouse and rat poisons

Collar and Leash

You will need an inexpensive collar and leash for your new puppy. A nylon one may be a better choice while the puppy is small. You will need to replace the collar several times before he stops growing, and nylon is generally less expensive. Puppies also like to chew on leather, so save the pretty leather collar for an adult Chihuahua who has outgrown the teething stage.

In preparation for walks and trips, accustom your dog to both the collar and the leash. For the collar, place it on the dog's neck and immediately feed him. He may scratch a little but will immediately become more interested in the food than in the collar. Leave the collar on for several minutes at a time until puppy gets used to it. Increase the collar-wearing time every day.

Next, pick up the leash and try guiding the Chihuahua around with a slight pressure on the leash. Puppy will buck, jump, and pull for a while, but will shortly get the hang of being guided on the leash with you in

control. The object here is for you to guide your dog—not vice versa.

Remember to continue with your praise when leash training your Chihuahua. It can be voice praise, patting praise, or tidbit reward. The earlier you begin training for the collar, leash and crate, the easier it will be to get the Chihuahua puppy to accept these things.

Never take your Chihuahua outside without a leash attached to the dog's collar with the proper animal identification tags on it!

Keep your puppy, or puppies in this case, in an uncarpeted area of the house where they can be near the family.

Bringing Your Puppy Home

Your Chihuahua should be at least eight weeks old before you take her home.

The best time of day to bring your new puppy home is in the morning. This will give you time to get acquainted and the puppy time to get acclimated to her new surroundings before bedtime. Weekends are best because the whole family will be home. Give the puppy freedom in a room where there is no carpet but lots of family activity. Her bed and crate can go into a corner of the room, along with a water dish and papers for "potty" training.

No one should rush at the puppy. Keep voices soft and calm. Give your puppy time to become acclimated to the new people and strange voices.

The First Night

The most difficult time will be the first night. This will probably be the puppy's first time away from mother and littermates.

The first night, puppy may whine or cry; do not be tempted to pick her up every time because this will only encourage her to whine for more attention. Play a radio quietly; a ticking clock near the puppy's bed will simulate the mother's heartbeat and may help calm the puppy. After a couple of nights, your Chihuahua will become accustomed to sleeping in her own bed or crate and will sleep through the night without a fuss.

Chihuahua Puppy Considerations

Do not grab at the puppy when you go to pick her up. Always pick up puppy with *two* hands, holding her firmly, but not too tightly, close to your body. Chihuahuas do not like to be held dangling in the air. Everyone in the family must be taught how to properly pick up and hold the Chihuahua. Place one hand under the chest and the other hand at the rear hindquarters. Do not stick your fingers between the rib cage and the fore limb (front leg) when you carry your Chihuahua. If you constantly hold your puppy in this manner, she will grow up to walk with elbows sticking out, and her front legs may grow to be crooked.

Treat your puppy with gentle reassurance, and she will soon grow used to her new home.

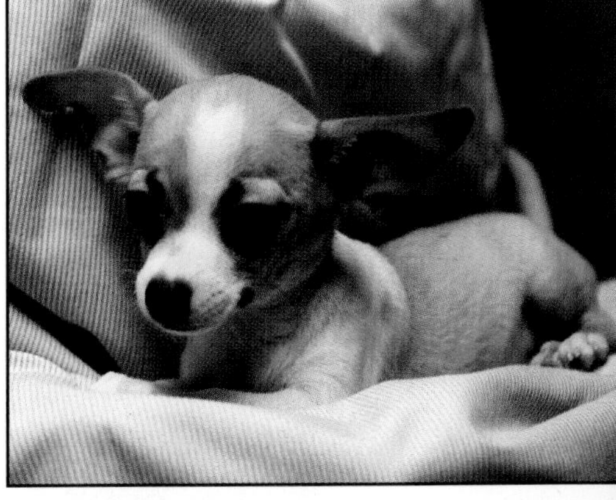

Children must be taught never to squeeze the Chihuahua. A squeeze could cause injury, and if squeezed too hard, the puppy might bite. Even the best-tempered dog will nip if hurt. Be certain to hold the puppy just snugly enough so that she does not fall out of your arms.

A Chihuahua puppy must never be placed in a spot where she could fall and injure herself. Do not leave a Chihuahua puppy alone on a chair or sofa; an adult Chihuahua will be able to jump off and on the furniture without injury, but a puppy will not.

Do not be concerned if the Chihuahua's ears are not erect at eight weeks of age. The ears will go up and down while puppy is teething. In some cases, especially if the ears are quite large, they may not become erect until puppy is five months old, at which time they may still flip-flop due to teething. If ears are not completely erect by six to seven months of age, they may never become erect.

HOUSEBREAKING

Housebreaking must be started as soon as puppy arrives home. You must decide whether to paper-train or train your puppy to go outdoors.

If you decide to paper-train, the puppy should be enclosed in a four- to five-foot area with bedding, toys, and water at one end of the enclosed area and several layers of paper at the other end. Paper-training will be necessary if you are away from the house for long periods. Puppies urinate often. Let puppy eliminate on the layers of paper, praise her, then remove the top layer of paper. A little of the urine will have soaked through, just enough to remind the puppy that this is where to potty.

Hold your Chihuahua gently but firmly, with one hand under the chest and the other supporting the hindquarters.

For a male puppy who will eventually learn to lift his leg to urinate, it will be necessary for him to have something to lift his leg on. For this purpose, crumple a wad of newspaper at least the size of a football and place it on top of the layers of papers at one end of the enclosed area. This pile will be his fire hydrant. Do not leave soiled papers around all day; it is not sanitary and will smell.

If you are planning outdoor housebreaking, then the puppy must be put on a schedule. Someone must be available at all times to take the puppy outside; puppies cannot wait! Go to the same spot each time. A young puppy of eight weeks may want to go out every hour. Older dogs can wait longer, but placing your Chihuahua on a schedule will make housebreaking easier.

If you began with paper-training, save some of the soiled paper and take it to the outside area you want to use for your dog to eliminate. She will quickly get the scent from the paper and then use that spot. Then out she goes to the same area, after every nap, after hard play, after every meal, in the middle of the morning and in the middle of the afternoon, after she has been left alone for a while, and finally, before everyone goes to bed at night. As the Chihuahua puppy gets older, this schedule can be adjusted and intervals between trips will become longer. An adult Chihuahua may only need to go out four or five times a day.

Never blame a puppy for having an accident in the house if you have forgotten to take her outside. Housebreaking can be achieved easily if you follow this routine and reward the Chihuahua with praise. *Never* stick your Chihuahua's nose into any urine or fecal matter. It is unhealthy for the dog, and it will teach her nothing. Do not hit or physically abuse your Chihuahua in any way. A stern vocal reprimand is better. Use a stern, calm voice for dog training, and do not shout or scream at the dog for making a mistake.

Do not allow your puppy the freedom of the house until you are absolutely certain she is housebroken. This may take only a few weeks, but on the other hand, it could take a couple of months. Many people like to keep puppy in the kitchen until she is house-reliable.

If you are unsure about feeding, training, or anything else pertaining to your new Chihuahua, do not hesitate to get in touch with the breeder, your veterinarian, or the training instructor. It is better to seek immediate information than to have some unfortunate incident occur that may prove harmful to your Chihuahua.

PUPPY ESSENTIALS

Your new puppy will need:

food bowl

water bowl

collar

leash

I.D. tag

bed

crate

toys

grooming supplies

Identification

The most common method of identification is a simple identification tag, inscribed with the owner's name and number and attached to the dog's collar. This method is easy, cheap and simple, but it is not sufficient. A collar can easily come off, or a tag can get lost. Consider another method of identification in addition to the ID tag.

One of the best means of permanent identification is a tattoo. Have your Chihuahua tattooed with her AKC registration number. You will be traced through the AKC's records. Tattooing can be done by your veterinarian and is fairly painless.

Another option is the microchip. These are extremely small devices encoded with necessary identification information. They are painlessly inserted under the skin by your veterinarian. If your dog is lost, a scanner is needed to "read" the microchip. Many veterinarians, animal shelters and humane societies already have these scanners. Even though this program is relatively new, thousands of pets are already enrolled. Until these scanners are universal, however, you may want to consider an additional method of identification as well.

Being a Good Neighbor

This is part of the responsibility of dog ownership. Your Chihuahua should not be allowed to wander around the neighborhood. The chance of her getting lost, killed by a car, poisoned, or stolen is very great. There are all kinds of poisonous substances your Chihuahua could swallow. She could pick up parasites. Your Chihuahua might be attacked by another animal, or worse yet, bitten by a rabid squirrel or raccoon. If your Chihuahua becomes frightened while on the loose, she might bite someone.

Many communities now have regulations concerning wandering and roaming pets. The laws may require that you have your dog on a leash when she is off your property. Some major cities have a curb law, which means you must clean up after your dog. Always carry some sort of plastic bag with you for this purpose.

Though your Chihuahua may be confined to a special area in your yard, she should not be left out for long periods, barking and carrying on. Your pet should not be noisy at six o'clock in the morning or ten o'clock at night. Noisy dogs do not make good neighbors.

Bringing An Older Chihuahua into Your Life

We have been discussing how to prepare and provide for a Chihuahua puppy in your life, but getting a puppy is not your only option. You may want to consider adopting an older Chihuahua providing he is sound physically.

Many irresponsible dog owners dispose of their dogs without consideration or compassion for the animal. As a result, many dog clubs have rescue programs. Members of the clubs take in unwanted or abandoned Chihuahuas, retrain them as needed, see that they are in good health and vaccinated, and prepare them for relocation to a caring, loving home.

Older dogs make equally good pets and may already be housebroken. Some are well versed in general good manners, so there may be quite an advantage in that respect. An older dog may require a little more patience in adjusting to a new environment, but no matter the age of the Chihuahua, the dog will be trainable for your house. Occasionally, rescue dogs are very young, but generally, the rescued Chihuahuas are four or more years old. These older Chihuahuas make wonderful pets and will still provide you with many years of happiness and companionship.

There is usually a request for a donation to the club's rescue fund to help offset the costs of retraining and health care. Give yourself a medal and a halo for adopting one of these abandoned Chihuahuas. If you select your older dog from a Chihuahua rescue service, follow the same sensible procedure you would when selecting a puppy from a breeder, and follow through on health maintenance, feeding and training.

chapter 5

Feeding Your Chihuahua

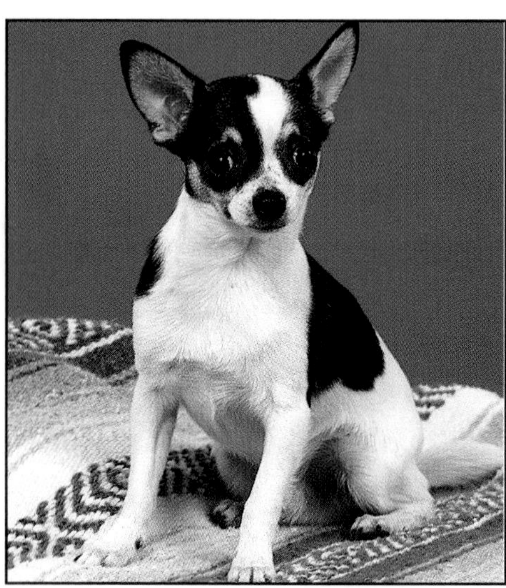

Keeping your Chihuahua on a well-balanced diet, avoiding constant and unnecessary treats, and maintaining a regular feeding schedule and exercise program will help keep your dog in top physical condition. The longer we keep our Chihuahuas in good health, the happier we are, for it means that our dogs will have longer and happier lives to share with us.

How Much to Feed Your Chihuahua

Before bringing home your new dog, ask for the puppy's feeding schedule and information about what and how much he is used to eating. Maintain this regimen for at least the first few days before gradually changing to a schedule that is more in line with the family's lifestyle. The breeder may supply you with a small quantity of the food the puppy has been eating. Use this or have your own supply of the same food ready when you bring home your puppy.

After the puppy has been with you for three days and has become acclimated to his new environment, you can begin a gradual food change. Add a portion of the new food to the usual food. Add a little more of the new food each day until it has entirely replaced the previous diet. This gradual change will prevent an upset stomach and diarrhea. The total amount of food to be fed at each meal will remain the same at this stage of the puppy's life.

Your puppy will be on four meals a day until you see that he's leaving food in the dish. At this point, he no longer needs four meals; it's now time to switch to three meals at equal intervals.

Your puppy will let you know when it is time to go to two meals a day, spaced about ten to twelve hours apart. Again, he will begin to leave food in the bowl on the three-meals-per-day schedule. Increase the portions given at each meal when you switch to two meals a day. It will take a little trial and error to determine how much food you should offer at each meal. Again, the dog should be fed at the same time each day.

TYPES OF FOODS/TREATS

There are three types of commercially available dog food—dry, canned and semimoist—and a huge assortment of treats (lucky dogs!) to feed your dog. Which should you choose?

Dry and canned foods contain similar ingredients. The primary difference between them is their moisture content. The moisture is not just water. It's blood and broth, too, the very things that dogs adore. So while canned food is more palatable, dry food is more economical, convenient and effective in controlling tartar buildup. Most owners feed a 25% canned/75% dry diet to give their dogs the benefit of both. Just be sure your dog is getting the nutrition he needs (you and your veterinarian can determine this).

Semimoist foods have the flavor dogs love and the convenience owners want. However, they tend to contain excessive amounts of artificial colors and preservatives.

Dog treats come in every size, shape and flavor imaginable, from organic cookies shaped like postmen to beefy chew sticks. Dogs seem to love them all, so enjoy the variety. Just be sure not to overindulge your dog. Factor treats into her regular meal sizes.

The puppy should receive a minimum of half a cup of food at each meal. If he still appears to be hungry, then increase the amount given at each meal. Each puppy is an individual, and just as members of your family eat different-sized portions, so will the individual Chihuahua.

If you have only one Chihuahua, buy the smallest bag of kibble you can find so it does not spoil.

Chihuahua puppies need four meals a day when they're very young.

What Nutrients Does Your Chihuahua Need?

Some of the nutrients your dog will need throughout his life are listed here. The amount of each nutrient will change according to the dog's age. A properly balanced diet will contain protein (extra protein for puppies and very active dogs), minerals, vitamins, and some fat, which should be polyunsaturated. There will be carbohydrates, but without excess salt. Food that does not have the sufficient amount of certain nutrients can affect your Chihuahua's growth and development. Likewise, too much of some nutrients may create problems just as serious. That is why the food must be balanced for the age and activity level of your individual dog.

Protein is necessary for bone growth and tissue healing.

Polyunsaturated fats keep the skin in tone and the coat shiny. Fat makes food tasty for dogs (and for humans). It is a source of concentrated energy and is needed as a carrier for fat-soluble vitamins. When dogs do not get enough fat, you will notice that the hair is dry, the skin is not soft, and muscle tone is deteriorating. On the other hand, too much fat is stored as body fat, too much of which is not good for the dog's health.

Carbohydrates provide energy.

Minerals play an important part in the dog's diet, working alongside vitamins to form enzymes that carry oxygen through the bloodstream.

Zinc is needed for a healthy coat and skin and also helps heal skin ailments and wounds. ***Calcium*** and ***phosphorus*** are necessary for bone growth, teeth, and the nervous system. These minerals are usually combined with ***vitamin D*** for quicker absorption. Calcium is also required for muscles and blood clotting. Although a deficiency in calcium is not uncommon, overuse of calcium can lead to kidney problems. ***Iron*** combined with vitamin B12 carries oxygen through the blood. ***Magnesium*** is for the nervous system and may prevent seizures. It also helps in the absorption of vitamins A, B and C, as well as calcium. ***Vitamin A*** is for skin, coat, growth, and eyes. ***Vitamin B*** is also for skin, eyes and coat, as well as the nervous system. ***Vitamin C*** is for blood and healing of tissues.

Though these vitamins and minerals are necessary for good health, more is not necessarily better. Do not give your Chihuahua supplements without consulting your veterinarian. Overuse of vitamins and minerals can harm your pet. (See the section on "Supplements" at

HOW TO READ THE DOG FOOD LABEL

With so many choices on the market, how can you be sure you are feeding the right food for your dog? The information is all there on the label—if you know what you're looking for.

Look for the nutritional claim right up top. Is the food "100% nutritionally complete"? If so, it's for nearly all life stages; "growth and maintenance," on the other hand, is for early development; puppy foods are marked as such, as are foods for senior dogs.

Ingredients are listed in descending order by weight. The first three or four ingredients will tell you the bulk of what the food contains. Look for the highest-quality ingredients, like meats and grains, to be among them.

The Guaranteed Analysis tells you what levels of protein, fat, fiber and moisture are in the food, in that order. While these numbers are meaningful, they won't tell you much about the quality of the food. Nutritional value is in the dry matter, not the moisture content.

In many ways, seeing is believing. If your dog has bright eyes, a shiny coat, a good appetite and a good energy level, chances are his diet's fine. Your dog's breeder and your veterinarian are good sources of advice if you're still confused.

the end of this chapter for more information on vitamins and minerals.)

Which Food Is Best?

Many food companies now produce different products for different stages of a dog's life. Different formulae are available for fat, old, young, and middle-aged dogs; foods high in protein for active animals, and less protein for sedentary dogs. There are even special foods for dogs with special medical problems.

Dry Food (Kibble)

To select a brand of commercial kibble, read the label to determine the ingredients. They are listed in order of quantity. There will also be a list of vitamins and minerals. Your dog's food is not a good thing on which to compromise. Choose a dog food with high-quality ingredients. Some substandard dog foods use animal by-products to maximize the amount of protein in the food. Much of this protein is useless because dogs can't digest it. Puppyhood is an especially crucial time, and quality ingredients are needed to insure that the bones, coat, skin, and every other physical and mental part of the dog are getting the proper nutrients. It is of equally vital importance that an owner not try to skimp on the portions of the quality nourishment, thinking that less food will help keep a dog small.

Your Chihuahua will thrive on high-quality kibble mixed with a small amount of canned food.

When your Chihuahua is placed on a two-meals-per-day regimen, one meal should consist of dry food soaked in hot water for five minutes (be sure it has cooled before feeding). Mix the moistened food with a rounded tablespoon, minimum, of canned food. The canned food should also be manufactured by a well-known dog food company. Check the ingredients rather than the price, and do not skimp on quality. Because you will only use a small amount of canned food at a time, buy small cans and keep them refrigerated once opened.

The second meal of the day should consist of dry food only. As the dog crunches up the food, the dry pieces will scrape against the teeth, helping keep them clean.

> **HOW MANY MEALS A DAY?**
>
> Individual dogs vary in how much they should eat to maintain a desired body weight—not too fat, but not too thin. Puppies need several meals a day, while older dogs may need only one. Determine how much food keeps your adult dog looking and feeling her best. Then decide how many meals you want to feed with that amount. Like us, most dogs love to eat, and offering two meals a day is more enjoyable for them. If you're worried about overfeeding, make sure you measure correctly and abstain from adding tidbits to the meals.
>
> Whether you feed one or two meals, only leave your dog's food out for the amount of time it takes her to eat it—10 minutes, for example. Freefeeding (when food is available any time) and leisurely meals encourage picky eating. Don't worry if your dog doesn't finish all her dinner in the allotted time. She'll learn she should.

Semimoist Food

Semimoist food is not recommended for your Chihuahua. I've found it makes the dog drink more water than usual. It is often filled with preservatives and food coloring and does nothing to prevent tartar buildup on teeth.

Water

Fresh, clean water must be available at all times. If the water dish is near dust or dirt, it may need to be cleaned and replenished more than once a day. Dogs who eat primarily dry kibble will probably drink more water. Thoroughly clean and rinse the water dish every day. Do not use any disinfectant to wash your Chihuahua's dishes. A new puppy owner was in the habit of disinfecting the water and food dishes, and although the owner could not smell the remaining odor, the Chihuahua could easily detect the smell. As a result the dog refused to drink or eat from the bowls and became dangerously dehydrated.

Treats and Scraps

For a treat once in a while, offer tiny dog biscuits. These come in small packages for small dogs, and help keep teeth clean. One or two a day is permissible, but do not substitute these biscuits for the dog's regular food or you may inadvertently encourage finicky eating habits in your dog.

Table scraps are permissible. Serve them only if cut, mashed, and blended thoroughly with the dog's regular food. Make the table scraps so small that they cannot be picked out from the regular dog food or you may inadvertently encourage finicky eating habits in your dog.

Weight Problems

If your pet has become a couch potato, the place to cut back is probably in the amount of fat and calories that the dog is consuming. If your Chihuahua is weighing in at twelve pounds and is only seven inches tall, he would be placed in the obese category! Carrying excess weight is bad for both the dog's heart and its limbs. If you cannot easily feel the ribs of the Chihuahua, he is most likely overweight.

Some older dogs have the opposite problem; these dogs are underweight. If the older dog is not suffering from a medical problem but is still underweight, try a premium dog food, that is packed with nutrients. Discuss this with your veterinarian. The condition and general health of the Chihuahua must be considered before any dietary changes for the older dog are made.

Forbidden Foods

Dogs love chocolate, but under *no* circumstances should your Chihuahua get even one small tidbit of it. Dogs cannot digest chocolate the way we can, although they love the taste just as much as we do. Some dogs have perished from an overdose of chocolate. Put a little sign on the chocolate box: "Hazardous to your dog's health!"

Do not feed the Chihuahua from your plate while you are dining. Table feeding will turn the dog into a table pest, which is annoying to you and embarrassing when you have company. This practice will also turn your Chihuahua into a finicky eater. This is unhealthy for your dog because he's not getting the nutrients he needs.

The Picky Eater

Allow your Chihuahua only ten minutes to eat his meal. If he has not finished in that time, take away the food and dispose of it. A dog that lingers over food for a half hour or more will tend to become a picky eater. There's no need to feel sorry for your dog. A healthy dog will eat before he starves.

Occasionally, a dog will "go off its feed" or, in other words, will not want to eat anything for a day or so. If the dog appears to be normal in all other respects, then he is probably all right. A visit to the veterinarian is warranted if the dog shows signs of illness or does not eat for three days.

If your Chihuahua becomes a finicky eater, it is probably your fault. Perhaps you have become lax in maintaining the feeding schedule because it does not fit your lifestyle. That is why it is so important that schedules be adjusted to the family's life as soon as possible.

Supplements

What are supplements, and should you give them to your Chihuahua? Veterinarians and breeders alike disagree about adding supplements to a puppy's diet. Many feel that if a good-quality food is offered, supplementation is not necessary. Others take a middle road. If the dog is a very good eater and is fed quality dog food, supplementation may not be needed; however, if puppy or adult dog is a nibbler or a picky eater, it may be necessary to supplement with vitamins and minerals.

There are many good quality puppy supplements on the market, and it is recommended that you discuss

the matter with your veterinarian before using any of these additions. The previously mentioned calcium and vitamin D product is readily available as a single tablet that dogs seem to like. Any change in your dog's diet requires a discussion with your veterinarian.

Feeding Your Older Chihuahua

Nutritional needs of older dogs will differ considerably from those of a puppy or adult. A small dog is usually considered to be in the geriatric range at about eleven years of age, although some pet food companies consider seven years of age to be senior. Small dogs live well into their late teens, and at this rate it is not unreasonable to consider eleven years of age as "senior citizenship."

Veterinarians today believe that the amount of protein in the dog's diet should decrease as the dog gets older. Excess protein may cause kidney ailments in older dogs.

It is up to you to feed your Chihuahua properly so that he remains in good physical condition, internally and externally. A nutritionally well cared for Chihuahua is a happy, healthy Chihuahua and will provide you with many years of faithful companionship.

chapter 6

Grooming Your Chihuahua

Good grooming techniques and a faithful grooming program will help keep your Chihuahua clean and in good physical condition.

Supplies

There are several items needed for good grooming care. Some of the most important are a hard rubber comb (not nylon or plastic), a natural bristle brush, baby shampoo, a medicated shampoo if there are skin problems, cotton balls, cotton swabs, nail clippers, mat splitter, toothbrush, tooth scaler, blow dryer, and cotton bath towels.

Before brushing, a thorough examination of the dog's skin is essential. Look for signs of external parasites, such as fleas or ticks, skin abrasions, bruises, and any other abnormalities like lumps or skin infections. If such things are found early, it is much easier to cure the problem.

The Chihuahua will not object to this examination; in fact, most like it. Check the dog's ears for discharge and unusual odors. If there is a black substance in the ear, the dog may have ear mites; this requires veterinary treatment. Take a sample of the ear discharge to your veterinarian so that the substance can be examined under a microscope and the correct medication prescribed.

Comb out ear fringe on the long-coated Chihuahua.

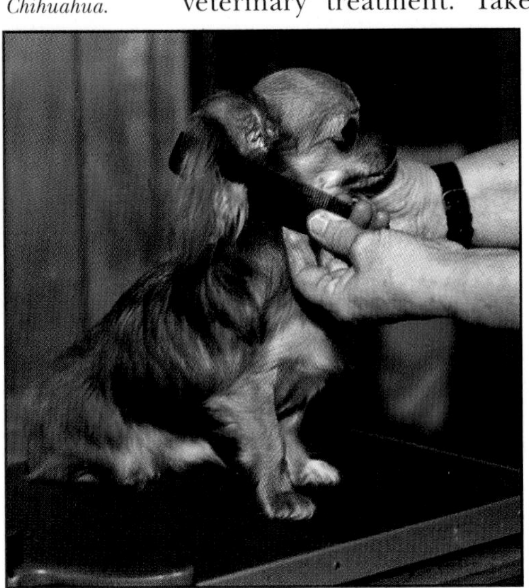

Run your hands all over the body; this will provide skin stimulation and an opportunity to find signs of abnormalities. This examination time will take less than five minutes. Your Chihuahua will love grooming time!

Brushing

A thorough brushing three times a week is absolutely necessary; daily brushing is even better. Frequent brushing means less hair around the house, and your Chihuahua will be cleaner and need fewer baths.

While going through the coat, look for mats; these are clumps of fine hair stuck together. If mats are a problem, particularly the very fine hairs of the ear fringe, you are not brushing often enough, or the dog is dirty.

A Chihuahua's coat grows in cycles. It will grow for a while, then stop, then dry out, and from there it will shed. It takes about 125 to 135 days to complete the cycle, on average, but this time frame will vary. Shedding takes place, usually in the spring, when dogs get rid of the winter coat, but because Chihuahuas are house dogs, they probably will not have a heavier winter coat, so shedding may occur at any time, depending on whether they keep close to the heat or air-conditioner ducts.

Grooming supplies must include a natural bristle brush, a toothbrush and nail clippers. Also shown here are nice collars and leashes.

No one likes to find dog hair all over the furniture or carpeting, especially a houseguest, but if this is occurring in your house, you are not caring for the Chihuahua's coat properly. That is why daily brushing is recommended. This will keep dog hair on the grooming brush and not on the furniture. Whether your Chihuahua is a long coat or a smooth coat, it is still necessary to have frequent brushings. It is much easier to pick up long coat hair on the furniture, but that smooth coat hair is like little spikes; it sticks into the clothing and furniture. Daily brushing not only gets out the dead coat that is shedding, but also stimulates new hair growth.

Brushing should begin the day after you get the puppy home. Do not delay. The longer you wait, the more difficult it will be to accustom the dog to a grooming program. The dog should be in your lap when brushing. Use a natural bristle brush on the body coat, and a hard rubber comb on the ear fringe, pants and leg fringes. The tail plume will take both a brush and a hard rubber comb. Nylon brushes and combs can cause static electricity, particularly if your house air is very dry (wintertime). Dogs will not like getting shocks from the nylon products.

With the dog in your lap, right side up, or on a nonslip table, with the head away from you and the rear end of the puppy toward your body, begin brushing by stroking in the direction opposite to the way the coat is growing, starting at the base of the spine. Going in the opposite direction for a few strokes gets out the dead hair quickly. Finish the routine by brushing in the direction that the coat is growing, from the back of the neck down the spine, along the body sides, toward the tail.

GROOMING TOOLS

pin brush

slicker brush

flea comb

towel

mat rake

grooming glove

scissors

nail clippers

tooth-cleaning equipment

shampoo

conditioner

clippers

Also, be sure to brush the underside of the dog. Turn the dog on her back while still in your lap, and brush the neck, chest and belly. Return the dog to her normal position in your lap (right side up). Now comb the fine hairs of the ear fringe, the leg furnishings and the pants with the hard rubber comb. If you find any mats, separate the hairs with a special tool called a mat splitter or separate each hair, little by little, until the mat is removed. The tail plume may be brushed first, then finished with the hard rubber comb. The entire brushing and combing should take about five minutes.

On a long coat, it may be necessary to trim just a little of the hair around the anus so the area can be kept clean during bowel movements. Do not trim unless the rear end constantly gets dirty.

Trimming Nails

In preparation for nail trimming, place the toes of each paw, one at a time, between your forefinger and your thumb, and exert a little gentle pressure so that puppy gets used to her toes being spread apart.

In a couple of days, try trimming the nails. Spread the toes, with your thumb on the pads of the foot and your forefinger on the top of the toes. Take off only the little hook at the end of the nail. Do not pull away on the nail clippers while cutting. You will see a little circle in the center of the end of the nail you have just clipped. This circle will get larger as you approach the quick of the nail. If you get too close to the quick, the nail will bleed, so be very careful. If the nail bleeds, a styptic pencil or an ice cube will stop the bleeding.

Trimming nails is an easy procedure for you and your Chihuahua if done quickly and carefully.

Some people prefer to grind down the nails with a Dremel tool, but the puppy must be exposed to this technique at a very early age; it is very noisy and vibrates on the nail, which can be frightening to a puppy. Also, take care not to get the grinder dust in the eyes or up the nostrils. Nail cutting and grinding should take place about every two weeks. The longer you wait to trim nails, the more resistant the puppy will get.

Bathing Your Chihuahua

It is not necessary to bathe a Chihuahua often unless he gets into something that is unusually dirty or smelly. A bath every month or two is generally sufficient under normal circumstances.

Although there are shampoos on the market specifically for dogs, it is quite in order to use a mild baby shampoo on your Chihuahua. These are called "tear free," but you must still be careful that no water or shampoo gets in the eyes or ears. To keep water from getting in the ears, place some cotton in the ear (not too far down), and do not forget to remove the cotton after the bath is complete. If your dog has skin problems, there are medicated shampoos for various skin conditions as well as for coat conditions.

Before beginning the bath, test the water on your wrist to be certain it is the correct temperature. Wet the coat thoroughly, taking care of ears and eyes. Rub the shampoo all over the dog's coat, and be sure to get to the underbelly, the tail plume, and all the fringes of the ears and legs. Then, rinse thoroughly; shampoo that remains in the dog's coat can lead to dandruff and itching and will also take away the shining glow of the coat.

Drying your Chihuahua

To dry the coat, use thick, all-cotton terry-cloth toweling for good water absorption. Pat dry to get out excess water. With another towel firmly but not roughly massage the coat. This will stimulate the skin as well as dry the coat. To complete the drying process, use a handheld blow dryer. Make sure it's not too hot, or it will burn the coat and skin. In the case of the long coat Chihuahua especially, blow dry in the direction that the coat grows—from the neck toward the tail. When the coat is thoroughly dry, run a finishing glove over the coat to give it an extra sheen.

For the long coat Chihuahua, use a hard rubber comb to comb ear and leg fringes and the tail plume. The reason for a hard rubber comb rather than a metal comb is that during dry weather, electric shocks can be prevented. The same is true for using a natural bristle brush. These particular grooming instruments are less apt to damage coat and fringes.

Ear Care

Check the ears every week to be sure they are in good condition. When ears are in good health, they are pink on the inside and the edges are free of splits or tears. There will be no odor emanating from the ears.

Cleaning the ears requires great caution. Use soft cotton ear swabs to clean only the part of the ear that you can see. Do not stick the swab down into the ear; this could result in serious injury.

If your Chihuahua constantly shakes her head, continually scratches her ears, or tilts her head to one side frequently, there may possibly be some kind of ear problem; a visit to the veterinarian is in order. Do not wait until the problem becomes serious.

Dental Hygiene

Dogs, too, need regular oral care for both gums and teeth. The American Veterinary Dental Society and the American Veterinary Medical Association promote good oral hygiene for pets. The AVDS states that 80 percent of dogs develop gum disease by three years of age. This organization believes that between veterinary dental checkups and proper home care, canine gum disease can be eliminated. Symptoms of gum disease are tartar around the gum line; swollen gums; red gums; bleeding gums; loose teeth; abscesses; and bad breath. Prevention is the first step. Have your veterinarian check for evidence of plaque; it can be kept under control by brushing several times per week.

Get your Chihuahua used to the toothbrush little by little.

Keeping teeth clean need not be a chore if proper techniques are begun while your Chihuahua is young. Get the puppy used to having her teeth brushed a minimum of three times per week. Brushing with plain warm, not hot, water is better than nothing, but canine toothpaste is available. Do not use a toothpaste made for humans; it will cause stomach upset.

Get your pet used to having her mouth opened and to your rubbing your fingers, or a soft gauze pad, gently over the gums. After a few days, when this routine is tolerated, begin to use a soft baby toothbrush. Start by just touching the toothbrush to the teeth. When puppy gets used to this, begin applying a little pressure. In a day or two, move the brush around the front of the teeth, gradually moving to the rear molars. Although it will not be puppy's favorite part of the grooming routine, she will learn to tolerate the brushing.

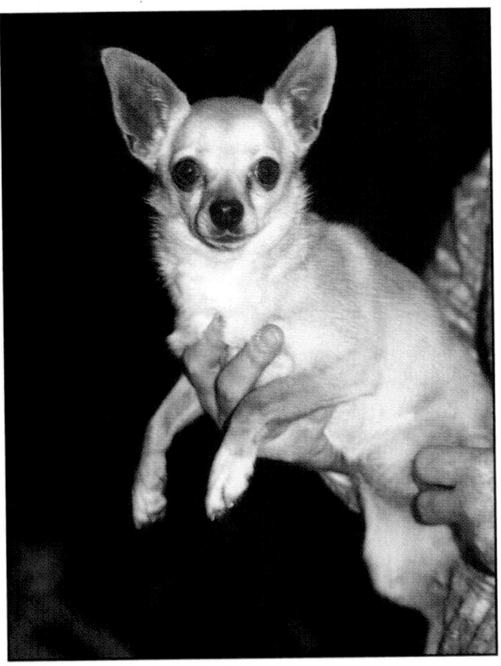
Tear staining may just be the result of small tear ducts, but it's best to check with your veterinarian.

If you do not brush often, a tooth scaler will be necessary. Get instructions from your veterinarian on how to use a scaler, because if it slips off the tooth, you might cut into the pet's gum. In fact, you may not be able to use a scaler at all, but a scaler will not be necessary if you stick to the frequent toothbrushing routine. This method is the least troublesome and the least costly for you. With patience it is not difficult to train your Chihuahua to accept the toothbrush method for cleaning teeth. A minimum of a once-a-year veterinary dental checkup is also in order. Rawhide bones, nylon bones, and other gnawing toys will help keep your Chihuahua's teeth clean.

Eye Care

Chihuahua eyes require little care. If your dog is susceptible to tear staining, the area under the eyes will be constantly wet. This may be due to small tear ducts, in which case there is little that can be done except to wipe and clean around the eyes daily with distilled water to prevent an accumulation of bacteria or dirt. In addition, if you see hair from the puppy's face poking into the eye, keep the hair trimmed. How a dog's eyes are constructed will have much to do with the cause of the tear staining. Dogs with full or more protruding eyes are more susceptible to tear staining.

More serious causes of tear staining include *entropia,* a condition caused by the eyelashes rubbing against the eye. Because the eyelashes constantly rub against the cornea, an ulcer may result. *Ectropia* is another name for a sagging lower eyelid. This will allow all sorts of dirt to enter the eye surface and may cause conjunctivitis. These two problems are not common to the Chihuahua.

As soon as you notice tear staining on your puppy's face, have your veterinarian perform an eye examination. There are veterinary specialists in ophthalmology, and your veterinarian may recommend one if the tear staining cannot be cured with the most common methods or medications. Daily eye care is a must for a dog who has constant tear staining.

chapter 7

Keeping Your Chihuahua Healthy

The easiest way to keep your Chihuahua healthy is to provide good preventive care and a healthy lifestyle. A complete series of vaccinations, heartworm preventive, and a one-time spaying or neutering procedure will give your Chihuahua a healthy start and keep him free of some of the most dangerous canine conditions. By providing your pet with daily grooming, good dental care, a nutritious diet and plenty of exercise, you are giving him the best assurance of a long and healthy life.

Always keep in mind that your Chihuahua is not only your pet and companion, but also your partner for a lifetime, his lifetime. With this attitude in mind, you will always take the right steps in the care and handling of your Chihuahua friend.

Choosing a Veterinarian

Choosing a veterinarian should be at the top of your priority list. Get recommendations from your breeder and other Chihuahua or small breed owners. Look for a veterinarian who specializes in the care of small dogs. Do not wait until your pet is sick to seek veterinary treatment. It would not be good for the dog, and it may be difficult for you to communicate with this stranger who is trying to treat your pet.

Alternative Medicine

If you are interested in holistic medicine, homeopathy or other nontraditional treatments, there are some veterinarians who practice this kind of medicine; others will practice both traditional western medicine as well as alternative medicine. These are listed in veterinary medical journals, or you can call the local veterinary society. Alternative animal treatments can provide you with many options for treating your Chihuahua.

Visiting the Veterinarian

Above all, your veterinarian should be able to get along with your pet and with you. You can help maintain this good relationship by keeping your appointments and by being on time. Always call if a change is necessary. Remember that everyone's time is important.

When you take your dog to the vet, ask questions about the diagnosis and treatment and how to care for your pet after she is brought home. Listen carefully to all directions regarding aftercare, feeding and administering medications. Write down everything so you will remember what to do when you get home.

Discuss fees frankly; you do not want to be surprised. Some veterinarians will accept credit cards; most will want payment of some kind at the time of the office visit, just as your own doctor does. Remember that this is a business and prompt payment is appreciated. If major surgery or long-term care is needed, get an estimate in advance and make financial arrangements.

Most veterinarians will have an answering service for emergencies. Make certain that it is an emergency, and do not call on a whim. The answering service will ask pertinent questions, but the individual anwering the phone is not medically trained. He or she will try to get the most important information so that the veterinarian can be informed about the emergency. Keep your telephone line free while waiting for the doctor to return your call. Do not go to the hospital without calling the answering service first especially if it is after hours. Your dog's life may depend on it. The doctor may want to give you preliminary instructions before proceeding with the trip to the animal clinic.

Puppies are especially susceptible to some of the worst diseases, so make sure you set a vaccination schedule and stick to it.

Preventive Care

Preventive medicine includes inoculations and booster shots for diseases, including distemper, hepatitis, leptospirosis, parvovirus and rabies. Your Chihuahua will also need preventative heartworm treatment and a one-time spaying or neutering procedure.

Vaccinations

For vaccinations and booster shots, it is recommended that Chihuahuas do not receive a multivaccination.

Chihuahuas have been known to have allergic reactions to multivaccinations given at the same time. With this in mind, set up a vaccination schedule with your veterinarian, and stick to it!

The age for vaccinations can best be determined by your veterinarian. Puppies must be fully weaned for several weeks in order for vaccines to be effective. It may be best to get rid of all internal and external parasites before vaccination takes place. Vaccinations are available for all the following infectious diseases. All the following diseases can be prevented by vaccinating your Chihuahua. Set up an immunization schedule with your veterinarian and stick to it.

YOUR PUPPY'S VACCINES

Vaccines are given to prevent your dog from getting an infectious disease like canine distemper or rabies. Vaccines are the ultimate preventive medicine: they're given before your dog ever gets the disease so as to protect him from the disease. That's why it is necessary for your dog to be vaccinated routinely. Puppy vaccines start at eight weeks of age for the five-in-one DHLPP vaccine and are given every three to four weeks until the puppy is sixteen months old. Your veterinarian will put your puppy on a proper schedule and will remind you when to bring in your dog for shots.

Distemper

This virus is widespread and very contagious, so you must protect your Chihuahua early in life. Symptoms are fever, seizures, diarrhea, coughing, and, possibly, watery discharge from the nose and eyes and convulsions. Distemper affects both the respiratory and the nervous systems and is often fatal.

Hepatitis

An adult dog may recover from this disease, but in a puppy it is very serious and often fatal. There can be damage to the eye as well as the liver and kidneys. Chronic illness may result. Symptoms are diarrhea, vomiting and a fever. There may be abdominal pain.

Leptospirosis

Dogs of any age can get this bacterial disease that damages many major organs. Symptoms are blood in the feces, fever, hemorrhage and jaundice. Your dog may appear completely exhausted.

Respiratory Infections

Kennel cough is a respiratory infection that is also known as tracheobronchitis. Although usually not fatal, it could develop into pneumonia, which can be. Symptoms are coughing, which may last for weeks, lack of pep and appetite loss. There are several stains of this disease and there are protective vaccines for many of them.

Parainfluenza is another highly contagious respiratory disease. In puppies the infection can be very severe. Symptoms are a dry, hacking cough. Sometimes this disease is mistaken for tracheobronchitis, as the symptoms are very similar. A vaccine for parainfluenza is usually administered in the puppy and adult series of immunizations, and is very effective.

When to Call the Vet

In any emergency situation, you should call your veterinarian immediately. You can make the difference in your dog's life by staying as calm as possible when you call and by giving the doctor or the assistant as much information as possible before you leave for the clinic. That way, the vet will be able to take immediate, specific action to remedy your dog's situation.

Emergencies include acute abdominal pain, suspected poisoning, snakebite, burns, frostbite, shock, dehydration, abnormal vomiting or bleeding, and deep wounds. You are the best judge of your dog's health, as you live with and observe him every day. Don't hesitate to call your veterinarian if you suspect trouble.

Parvovirus

Parvovirus is highly contagious and very often results in death. Symptoms are vomiting and bloody diarrhea. It is very serious in puppies.

Coronavirus

Coronavirus causes viral diarrhea and affects both puppies and adult dogs. Symptoms are loss of appetite combined with weight loss, vomiting diarrhea, listlessness and excessive thirst.

Rabies

Rabies is transmitted by the bite of an infected animal. This virus attacks the nerve tissues and is very contagious to both humans and animals; if left untreated, the result is paralysis and death. Today's rabies vaccination programs are much improved, and there has been an increase in public education and awareness of this disease. All states require rabies vaccinations for pets, and these shots must be kept up to date.

To help control rabies, do not feed or adopt wild animals; keep the outside garbage pail covers on tightly; do not leave food outside; and above all, do not allow your Chihuahua to roam the neighborhood or stay in the backyard unattended. Contact your veterinarian immediately if you think your Chihuahua has been bitten by a wild animal.

Parasites

Parasites are a fact of life for dogs. It is up to you to control them and keep your dog free of the diseases they may carry. Cleanliness is the way to start. This includes the exterior of the animal and your puppy's bedding and entire environment, including your house and your yard.

Signs of internal parasites include weight loss and an unusually rounded belly. If you notice these symptoms, take a stool specimen to your veterinarian. Do not confuse a full belly after a meal with the constantly rounded belly of a puppy with internal parasites.

Internal Parasites

Heartworm

When a mosquito bites a dog with heartworms, the mosquito becomes the carrier and transfers the infection to the next dog that it bites. As the heartworms develop, they migrate to the dog's heart. Heartworms have been known to grow as long as fourteen inches! Heartworms cause lung and permanent heart damage and may even cause death. Treatment can be costly as well as dangerous. Symptoms are coughing, breathing difficulty, weight loss and lethargy. Preventive medication, administered daily or monthly, is available in tablets or chewable

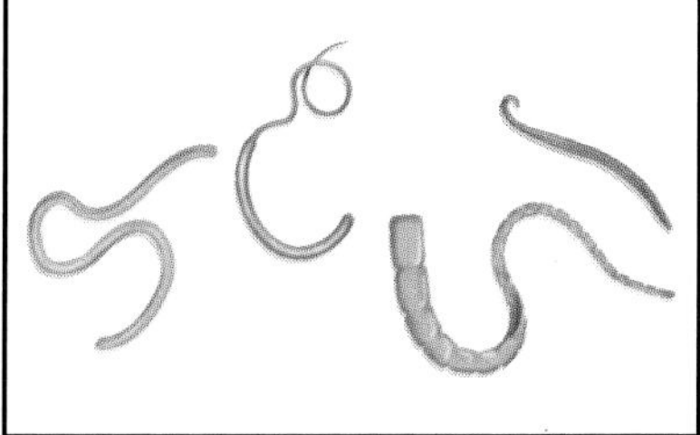

Common internal parasites (l-r): roundworm, whipworm, tapeworm and hookworm.

chunks that dogs seem to like. Early veterinary diagnosis can save the life of your Chihuahua. Do not be misled because Chihuahuas are house dogs; mosquitoes are everywhere, indoors and outdoors!

Roundworms

It is not unusual for a puppy to be born with roundworms because this internal parasite is passed from mother to offspring before the puppies are born. In egg form the roundworm is passed to other dogs from feces. The intestine is the home for roundworms, and these creatures can grow to be seven inches long. Symptoms of roundworms are dull coat, diarrhea, vomiting and a pot-bellied appearance. Liver and lung damage might occur, as well as pneumonia.

Hookworm

Hookworms are passed to puppies through mother's milk. They are smaller but much more dangerous than roundworms and can lead to a Chihuahua puppy's death within weeks. Hookworms suck blood from the intestines. In egg form, hookworm is transferred through feces. Through this route, the hookworms get into the bloodstream and wiggle their way to the intestines. Symptoms are anemia, weakness and weight loss and diarrhea.

Whipworms

Whipworms are a couple of inches long and live in the bowels. Dogs pick them up from infected soil. Puppies with whipworm appear sickly, thin and may have diarrhea.

Tapeworm

Fleas act as a host for tapeworms. When your dog bites at an itchy flea bite, he ingests the tapeworm. Puppies may have either diarrhea or constipation. There may be a marked increase in appetite.

All worming medications are dangerous and must be used only in consultation with a veterinarian. In addition to veterinary medications, parasites can be eliminated through strict sanitary conditions maintained where the dog eliminates and through periodic stool checkups to see if worming medication is needed.

Giardia

This parasite is actually a protozoan that gets into your dog's system through infected drinking water. Giardia invades the intestinal tract and the primary symptom is diarrhea. Small dogs, like the Chihuahua, and puppies are particularly susceptible. These parasites are common to wild animals in many areas, so if you have been out walking with your Chihuahua in a wild area and he develops diarrhea, suspect giardia. Make sure to see your veterinarian for diagnosis and treatment.

If you are outside away from home, it's a good idea to bring along drinking water for your Chihuahua. Even if the water's not contaminated, some dogs may avoid drinking water they're not used to because it smells or tastes slightly different. Also, avoid taking your dog to unsanitary places where lots of dogs congregate. These sites are breeding grounds for all kinds of pests.

FIGHTING FLEAS

Remember, the fleas you see on your dog are only part of the problem—the smallest part! To rid your dog and home of fleas, you need to treat your dog *and* your home. Here's how:

- Identify where your pet(s) sleep. These are "hot spots."
- Clean your pets' bedding regularly by vacuuming and washing.
- Spray "hot spots" with a non-toxic, long-lasting flea larvicide.
- Treat outdoor "hot spots" with insecticide.
- Kill eggs on pets with a product containing insect growth regulators (IGRs).
- Kill fleas on pets per your veterinarian's recommendation.

External Parasites

Recent research in flea and tick control has brought forth some new means of controlling and preventing this common problem. Some flea and tick prevention and management programs are available only through veterinary supervision and treatment, while others are over-the-counter products. These flea and tick management programs can usually get rid of, or at least control, this problem, by breaking the infestation cycle of the parasite.

Fleas

Flea bites are irritating and can cause itchy red skin on both humans and dogs. Flea bites may cause an allergic reaction. Fleas often transmit tapeworm to dogs. To keep fleas under control, they must be eliminated from your dog and the home environment, inside and out, as well as from your car interior if your dog travels with you. Many flea sprays and flea bombs are available for this purpose.

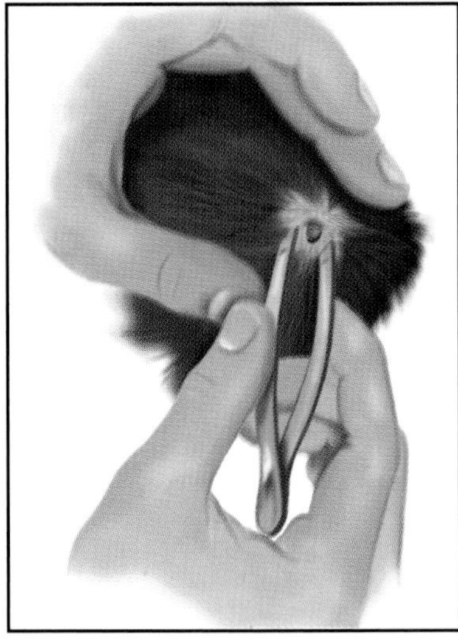

Use tweezers to remove ticks from your dog.

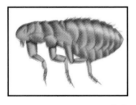

To keep fleas at bay on your dog, there are dips, shampoos and collars, but the best program for flea extermination is one that comes from your veterinarian. For each flea that you actually see, there are at least a dozen that you do not. A female flea can lay many thousands of eggs. Fleas can live for several months, hopping off and on your dog, in and out of the dog's living quarters, as well as in the backyard or any other place your dog may go. The best means to get rid of fleas is to attack them while they are just beginning to develop and to interrupt their life cycle. New drugs are available through your veterinarian that do just this. Your dog takes just one tablet per month, and the medication stops the fleas' growth cycle. Giving medication is much easier than bathing or dipping the dog with an insecticide and is a great deal safer.

It is best, though, to begin flea management before you see even one flea. This can be done through using special sprays for your house and for the immediate area outside of the house, in addition to doing whatever your veterinarian recommends.

The flea is a die-hard pest.

Ticks

Ticks carry Lyme disease and other ailments such as Rocky Mountain spotted fever, which can affect dog and human alike. The deer tick that carries Lyme disease is extremely tiny and may not be readily visible to the naked eye.

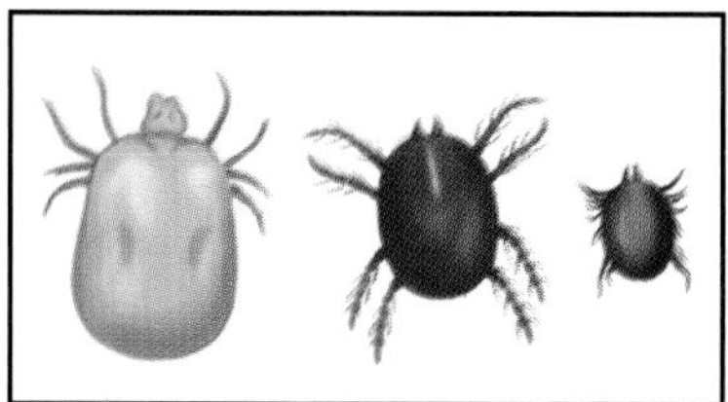

Three types of ticks (l-r): the wood tick, brown dog tick and deer tick.

If you should see a tick on your dog, first soak the tick in alcohol, then very carefully pull it out with a pair of tweezers. Do not touch the tick with your fingers because if it is carrying a disease, you could become infected. After pulling out the tick, you may notice that the head is still embedded under the skin. It will most likely fall off in a few days.

Mange

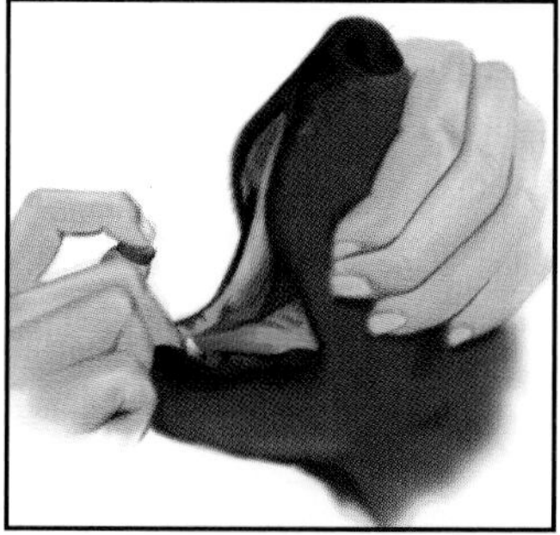

To give a pill, open the mouth wide, then drop it in the back of the throat.

Mange is caused by a mite and is recognized by hair loss; there is usually some skin lesion. Depending on the type of mange, the hair loss will either start at the head and ears or somewhere on the body, and it can easily spread. Mange can be a very serious condition if not treated promptly. There are all kinds of shampoos, ointments, dips and drugs available today to control the mange mite. Although mange is not a common problem, it is more apt to show up in puppies than in adult dogs.

Medical Procedures

To Give a Pill

To give a Chihuahua a pill, place the pill between your thumb and forefinger. Open the dog's mouth with your other hand (you will need someone to hold the Chihuahua during this procedure), and place the pill as far back as possible on the center of the tongue, toward the middle of the throat. Close the dog's mouth and tilt the head upward. Hold the mouth closed, but do not cover the nostrils. The dog should swallow the pill immediately. Check inside the mouth to be sure the pill has been swallowed.

Liquid Medication

Place the liquid in an eyedropper. Lift the Chihuahua's lips and put the eyedropper at the back corner of the mouth, forming a pocket with the lips. Close the lips and hold the head upright, squeezing out the liquid from the eyedropper. Hold the muzzle and the dog will swallow. It is easier to give a dog liquid medications than pills.

Ointment

Make sure you hold your Chihuahua firmly, in case he jerks, so the tube doesn't poke his eye. To apply eye ointment, pull the lower lid out and squeeze the correct amount of medication into the pocket formed by the lower lid. When the dog blinks, the ointment will be distributed around the eye.

Applying skin ointment is very simple; just spread the dog's fur and apply the ointment directly to the skin as best you can. If the area is infected or raw, be extra gentle and careful.

Squeeze eye ointment into the lower lid.

Applying the ointment may be simple, but the real challenge is making sure it stays on your Chihuahua. His first instinct will probably be to lick it off, further irritating the wound and eliminating any benefits of the medication. To prevent this, your vet may suggest he wear an **Elizabethan collar,** a protective collar named for its similarity to the fashion of Elizabeth I's reign. This large, cone-shaped collar will prevent your Chihuahua from licking off the medication and bothering the affected area. He will probably hate this clumsy device and seem very miserable, but try to get him to keep it on. Otherwise, the wound will take much longer to heal and he is risking serious infection.

Muzzle

To prevent being bitten while immobilizing a dog with broken bones, a temporary muzzle can be made with gauze bandage. Be certain that the muzzle restraint is not too tight and that the dog can breathe easily. The dog should be able to open the mouth a little. Keep the dog covered with a lightweight blanket.

Use a scarf or old hose to make a temporary muzzle, as shown.

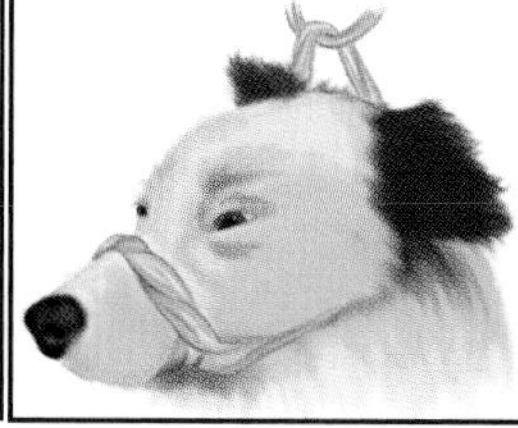

Taking Your Dog's Temperature

At some time or other you may need to take your Chihuahua's temperature because that is one of the first questions your veterinarian will ask you when you call. Taking your Chihuahua's temperature is not difficult. Use only a rectal thermometer that has a stubby, somewhat rounded end. Shake it down below 90 degrees Fahrenheit, coat the end with petroleum jelly, and insert the thermometer into the rectum with great caution, to about one to one and one half inches.

Hold the standing dog tightly so that he does not wriggle out of your grasp or try to sit, because the thermometer might break or become lodged too high in the rectum. An average temperature will be about 101.5 degrees Fahrenheit but may be slightly above or slightly below. A wide variation above or below requires veterinary attention. Your dog is sick!

Spaying and Neutering

For the health of your pet and your peace of mind, have your female spayed and your male neutered. Both procedures are usually done between six and twelve months.

Spaying your female is desirable for many reasons. From a health standpoint, she will not be susceptible to diseases of the reproductive organs, including pytometra, a life-threatening uterine infection, or vaginal prolapse, a painful and dangerous condition. If she is spayed at a young age, her risk of mammary cancer will be greatly reduced.

If you spay your female, you will not have male dogs incessantly hanging around the property, becoming a nuisance when the female is in season. You will not have to worry about bloody discharge staining the furniture or car.

Neutering your male will eliminate his risk of testicular cancer and may reduce the incidence of urinary tract infections. It will reduce his desire to roam in search of females in heat and will make him a more well-adjusted house pet.

It is not wise to have a litter just because you want your children to witness a birth. The children will lose interest in about two minutes, while the birth may take several hours and is very messy. When your children discover how much work is involved in tending a litter of puppies, the job will fall on the shoulders of the parents, usually Mom!

Spaying and neutering will keep more unwanted puppies from filling up the animal shelters. Hundreds of thousands of dogs, including Chihuahuas, are euthanized each year because there are not enough homes for all of them. Yes, even little dogs like Chihuahuas are dumped into the animal shelters. Chihuahuas have been abandoned in all kinds of

ADVANTAGES OF SPAY/NEUTER

The greatest advantage of spaying (for females) or neutering (for males) your dog is that you are guaranteed your dog will not produce puppies. There are too many puppies already available for too few homes. There are other advantages as well.

ADVANTAGES OF SPAYING

No messy heats.

No "suitors" howling at your windows or waiting in your yard.

Decreased incidences of pyometra (disease of the uterus) and breast cancer.

ADVANTAGES OF NEUTERING

Lessens male aggressive and territorial behaviors, but doesn't affect the dog's personality. Behaviors are often owner-induced, so neutering is not the only answer, but it is a good start.

Prevents the need to roam in search of bitches in season.

Decreased incidences of urogenital diseases.

weather by people who do not care about and feel no responsibility toward a dog they have acquired. Do not become a part of this cycle by breeding irresponsibly.

Problems Particular to the Chihuahua

The Chihuahua is fortunate in that the breed does not have a great many defects or problems. Breeders work hard to eliminate the defects that do exist, but no matter how diligent a breeder is, problems may creep in once in a while.

The Chihuahua is a healthy, long-lived breed.

Molera (Fontanel)

The molera, also referred to as the fontanel, is a soft spot at the top of the skull, very similar to a baby's soft spot. Sometimes it will disappear completely, though usually it does not. In a puppy, the molera is enlarged and will gradually grow smaller as the puppy matures, though it may never completely disappear. If it remains about the size of a dime, there is nothing to worry about; just avoid heavy-handedness while patting the skull. If the molera is excessively large on the skull of an adult or a puppy, there may possibly be a health problem related to hydrocephalus especially if the extraordinarily large molera is accompanied by other symptoms.

The molera is *not* a defect in the breed, but a unique *characteristic* of the breed. As far we know, the

Chihuahua is the only breed that may have this trait and still be a perfectly healthy dog. According to the breed standard, the Chihuahua may or may not have a molera; 80 percent to 90 percent of Chihuahuas do.

Hydrocephalus

This ailment is sometimes referred to as water on the brain. The head may be excessively large, usually due to swelling. Other symptoms are unsteadiness when walking, frequent falling, eyes that look in opposite directions (also known as east-west eyes), lots of white showing around the eyeballs and seizures. Puppies or adults with these symptoms usually do not live long. If the Chihuahua shows all the signs of hydrocephalus, it is more humane to have the dog "put to sleep" than to have it go through a limited life span in this painful condition.

Run your hands regularly over your dog to feel for any injuries.

Subluxation of the Patella

This condition is also known as slipping stifles (kneecaps). With this problem, the kneecap does not glide smoothly along the groove, but slips out from time to time. In a severe case surgery can help correct the problem. In mild cases surgery is not recommended because the dog will be able to live a relatively normal life, though he may not be an active jumper. Arthritis may develop as the dog ages, but it is apt to occur even in a dog with perfectly normal kneecaps. Subluxation of the patella appears in many small breeds.

Heart Murmur

Occasionally, a Chihuahua will develop a heart murmur, but just as in humans, the dog can usually lead a normal existence and a long life. This is not a very common problem in the breed.

Cleft Palate

Once in a while, a dog is born with a hole in the roof of the mouth, called a cleft palate. Dogs with this problem are unable to eat, so when this condition is discovered in a young puppy, the dog should be humanely euthanized.

Hypoglycemia

Low blood sugar is known as hypoglycemia. It will usually occur in very young puppies. Quite often a puppy will outgrow the condition and live a perfectly normal life. The symptoms are rigidness or limpness, unsteady gait, and seizures that may turn to unconsciousness. Sometimes, the symptoms last only a few seconds, though they may last as long as several minutes. Try to get some kind of sugar and water mixture into the animal's mouth, but take care that the puppy does not choke on the substance. It is imperative that immediate veterinary help be sought. Although not a common problem in the breed, it is mentioned here so that you will recognize the symptoms and take immediate corrective action.

Eye Injuries

Because of their slightly protruding eyes, Chihuahuas can be prone to eye injuries. If your Chihuahua injures an eye, flush it out for several minutes using water or a saline solution. This treatment may be sufficient, but if not, transport the dog to a hospital.

Anesthesia

Breeders of small dogs always worry about shock or even death from anesthesia. It is highly recommended

A FIRST-AID KIT

Keep a canine first-aid kit on hand for general care and emergencies. Check it periodically to make sure liquids haven't spilled or dried up, and replace medications and materials after they're used. Your kit should include:

Activated charcoal tablets

Adhesive tape (1 and 2 inches wide)

Antibacterial ointment (for skin and eyes)

Aspirin (buffered or enteric coated, *not* Ibuprofen)

Bandages: Gauze rolls (1 and 2 inches wide) and dressing pads

Cotton balls

Diarrhea medicine

Dosing syringe

Hydrogen peroxide (3%)

Petroleum jelly

Rectal thermometer

Rubber gloves

Rubbing alcohol

Scissors

Tourniquet

Towel

Tweezers

that anesthesia be given only when necessary. Because of the potential harmful effects of anesthesia, small dog owners need to be especially diligent about practicing good dental hygiene on their Chihuahuas, thus making teeth cleaning under anesthesia unnecessary.

To begin with, select a veterinarian or animal clinic with modern equipment and a staff that is knowledgeable about the latest methods of administering anesthesia.

Impacted Anal Glands

Impacted anal glands may be a problem. If you see your Chihuahua constantly scooting along the ground on his rear end or trying to lick himself around the anus, the anal glands may be impacted. Have your veterinarian show you how to empty these sacs; otherwise, a trip to the veterinarian may be needed about every six months to take care of this problem. If the anal sacs are not emptied regularly, infection may occur and surgery may be required.

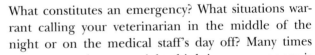

Common Medical Problems and First Aid

What constitutes an emergency? What situations warrant calling your veterinarian in the middle of the night or on the medical staff's day off? Many times what you might think is an emergency is only panic on your part. You certainly do not want to appear to be a dumbbell or to incur considerable expense if the medical matter is not a true emergency. Real emergencies will involve breathing difficulties, allergic reactions, paralysis, uncontrollable bleeding, broken limbs, a state of shock, bloat, urinary obstruction, seizures, uncontrollable diarrhea, vomiting and poisonings. Although the list of conditions that could be considered emergencies seems long, most do not occur often. Study the list of conditions below to help determine what constitues

An Elizabethan collar keeps your dog from licking a fresh wound.

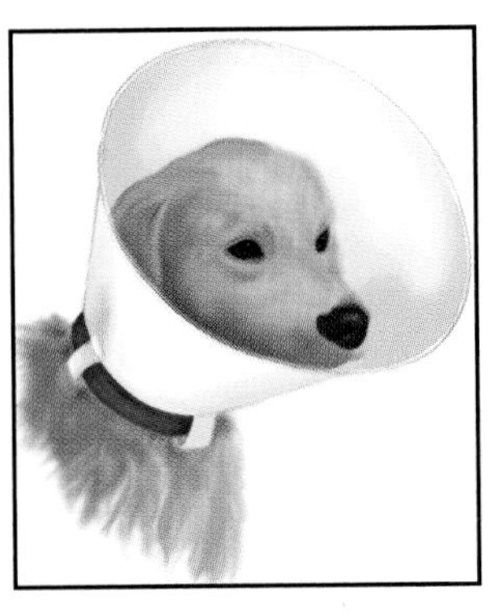

an emergency and what you can safely treat at home. Of course, if you are ever in doubt, call the vet or emergency care facility.

Many of the precautions, procedures and first-aid treatment for humans can be adapted for the care of your Chihuahua. Use common sense.

Appetite Loss

A Chihuahua will sometimes refuse to eat for a day or two. If the dog appears to be active, is drinking a normal amount of water, is sleeping as usual, and appears to be normal in every other respect, there is most likely nothing to worry about. If other symptoms appear, such as looking at the water in the bowl but not drinking; lethargy, vomiting, or diarrhea, get immediate veterinary care. Occasionally, a dog will eat some grass and immediately vomit; this is nothing to worry about and happens often.

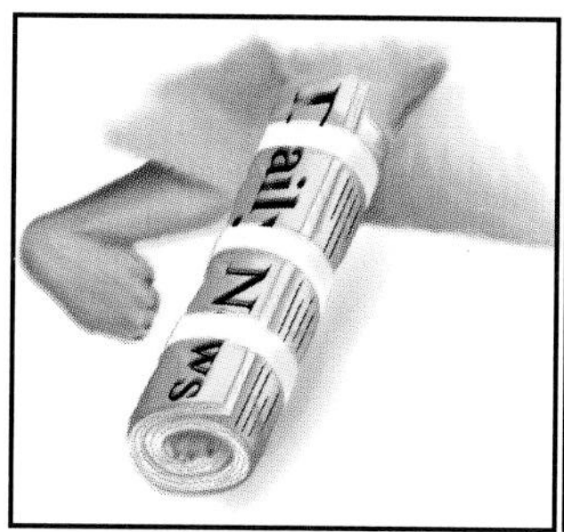

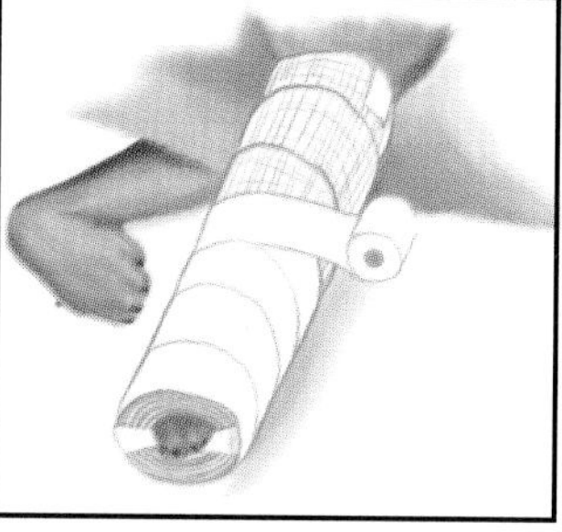

Make a temporary splint by wrapping the leg in firm casing, then bandaging it.

Broken Bones

If your dog breaks a bone, immobilize the limb very carefully, and seek veterinary help right away. If you suspect a spinal injury, place the dog on a board very slowly and carefully tie him securely to the board before immediately transporting him to the veterinarian.

Dehydration

To test your dog for dehydration, take some skin between your thumb and forefinger and lift the skin upward gently. If the skin does not go back to its original position quickly, the Chihuahua may be

suffering from dehydration. Consult your veterinarian immediately.

DIARRHEA

Diarrhea can be very serious or can simply indicate an upset stomach. If your Chihuahua has no other symptoms and has recovered in a day, he probably just ate something strange.

However, in very small puppies diarrhea can lead to dehydration and death, so react quickly in obtaining medical treatment. Diarrhea can be the result of many things, and the cause must be pinpointed by the veterinarian. Two of the most serious causes of diarrhea are canine parvovirus and canine coronavirus. If diarrhea continues more than twenty-four hours, if it is bloody, or if you notice other symptoms, call your veterinarian immediately.

POISONING

Vomiting, breathing with difficulty, diarrhea, cries of pain, and abnormal body or breath odor are all signs that your pet may have ingested some poisonous substance. Poisons can also be inhaled, absorbed through the skin, or injected into the skin, as in the case of a snakebite. Poisons require professional help without delay! Call the National Animal Poison Control Center hotline at (900) 680-0000. The call will be charged to your phone—$20.00 for the first five minutes and $2.95 for each additional minute.

Some of the many household substances harmful to your dog.

SCRATCHES AND CUTS

Minor skin irritations, such as scratches, can usually be cured by using an over-the-counter antibiotic cream or ointment. For minor skin problems, many ointments suitable for a baby work well on a Chihuahua.

Heatstroke

Heatstroke can quickly lead to death. *Never* leave your dog in a car, even with the windows open, even on a cloudy day with the car under the shade of a tree. Heat builds up quickly; your dog could die in a matter of minutes. Do not leave your Chihuahua outside on a hot day especially if no shade or water is provided.

Heatstroke symptoms include collapse, high fever, diarrhea, vomiting, excessive panting and grayish lips. If you notice these symptoms, you need to cool the animal immediately. Try to reduce the body temperature with towels soaked in cold water; massage the body and legs very gently. Fanning the dog may help. If the dog will drink cool water, let him. If he will not drink, wipe the inside of his mouth with cool water. Get the dog to the nearest veterinary hospital. Do not delay!

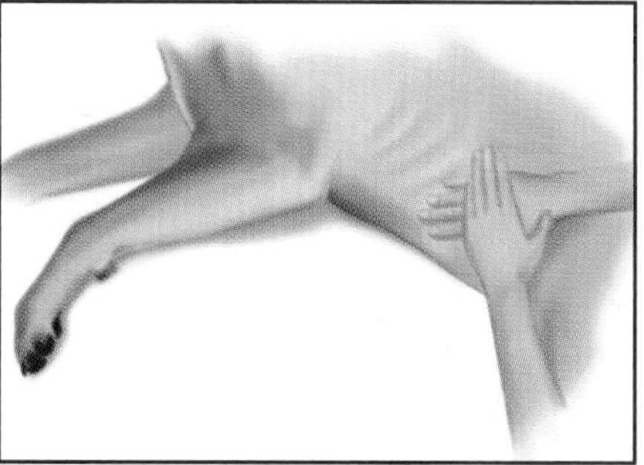

Applying abdominal thrusts can save a choking dog.

Bee Stings

Bee stings are painful and may cause an allergic reaction. Symptoms may be swelling around the bite and difficulty breathing. Severe allergic reaction could lead to death. If a stinger is present, remove it. Clean the bitten area thoroughly with alcohol; apply a cold compress to reduce swelling and itching and an anti-inflammatory ointment or cream medication. Seek medical help.

Choking

Puppies are curious creatures and will naturally chew anything they can get into their mouths, be it a bone, a twig, stones, tiny toys, string or any number of things. These can get caught in the teeth or, worse, lodged in

the throat and may finally rest in the stomach or intestines. Symptoms may be drooling, pawing at the mouth, gagging, difficulty breathing, blue tongue or mouth, difficulty swallowing and bloody vomit. If the foreign object can be seen and you can remove it easily, do so. Otherwise, rush to the veterinarian; surgery may be necessary to save your Chihuahua's life.

Bleeding

For open wounds, try to stop the bleeding by applying pressure to the wound for five minutes using a sterile bandage. If bleeding has not stopped after this time, continue the pressure. Do not remove the pad if it sticks to the wound because more serious injury could result. Just place a new sterile bandage over the first, and apply a little more pressure to stop the bleeding. This procedure will usually be successful. Take the dog to the medical center for treatment especially if the bleeding cannot be controlled rapidly.

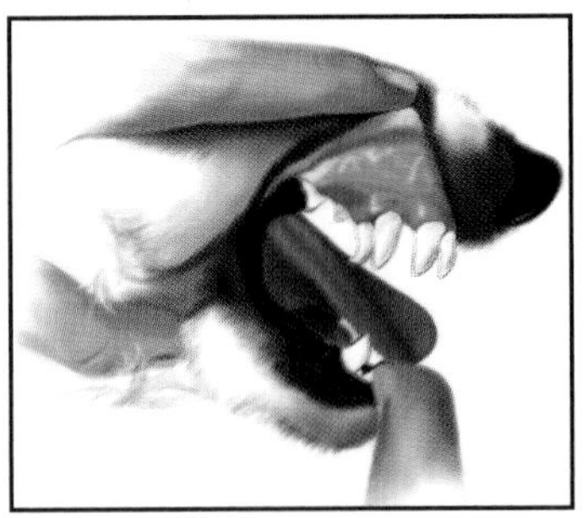

Check your dog's teeth frequently and brush them regularly.

If bleeding cannot be stopped with pressure, try pressing on the upper inside of the front leg for bleeding of that limb; for the rear limbs, press on the upper inside of the rear leg; for tail bleeding, press on the underside of the tail at its base. Do not attempt to stop the bleeding with a tourniquet unless the bleeding is profuse and cannot be stopped any other way. A tourniquet must be tight, consequently, it can not be left on for a long time because it will stop the circulation. It could be more dangerous than the bleeding!

Burns

Do not put creams or oils on a burn. Cool water can be used to carefully wash the burn area. Transport to the veterinary clinic immediately.

On the Mend

If your Chihuahua is ill or on the mend from some illness and cannot tolerate his usual diet of dry kibble and canned meat, try a blander diet for a few days.

Try mixing some Esbilac (a liquid milklike substance for dogs available at most pet supply stores) with strained chicken (baby food) and baby rice cereal. The latter two are available from the baby food department of the supermarket. Add a little vitamin supplement to help get your dog back to good health.

This smooth creamy mixture is something that dogs like, and it is easy to digest. As the dog begins to feel better, get him back to regular food gradually by adding it to the soft creamy diet; a little more each day until the Chihuahua is in improved health and back on his regular dog food diet.

Offer Support

You can help your dog deal with illness, pain or stress by comforting your dog with calm and soothing words. Petting the dog and talking to him quietly can help to lower heart rate and decrease stress. If the dog must be hospitalized for a long period, try to visit him daily. A visit from you and perhaps a favorite toy that you have brought along will help speed recovery. There is no question that good mental health can lead to good physical health for your Chihuahua.

Your Senior Citizen Chihuahua

If your Chihuahua is in good health, the first signs of advanced age will be white hairs appearing on the muzzle and around the eyes. The white hair may be accompanied by tooth loss and a preference for sleep over exercise.

As your Chihuahua advances in age and physical health is on the decline, some changes will have to be made in the dog's routine. There may be a need for dietary alterations. (*See* Chapter 5, "Feeding Your Chihuahua.") The older dog will need to be kept

warm and out of drafts, even more so than a Chihuahua puppy, because he will become chilled more easily.

Older dogs are subject to arthritis, so your Chihuahua may no longer be able to jump up onto the sofa. Therefore, place some kind of bedding in his favorite part of the house where he can cozy up during the day. If your older dog has been trained to go potty outside, he may no longer be able to go up and down stairs, so you may have to build a ramp for your pet.

Good grooming, good food, and good health care all contribute to winning style, in or out of the show ring.

The older Chihuahua may become a little crotchety, but that may be because he cannot hear or see as well as he used to. It may also be because his joints are not as nimble and arthritis may make them painful. There may be heart or kidney problems. Tooth loss may occur, making it more difficult to crunch the kibble. In that case it will be necessary to switch to a softer food.

Remember to give the older Chihuahua a great deal of affection, to provide comfort, and to make his life easy and enjoyable. Do not force him to do things that are more appropriate for a young puppy.

The older Chihuahua will become more set in his ways, so try not to make sudden adjustments in his daily routine, and do not move his bed to a new location; the dog may not be able to find it. The senior Chihuahua will still need exercise, but not as vigorous as he had as a puppy. Try to keep your older dog trim, with less strenuous exercise and a diet with fewer calories and less fat. Do not let your older Chihuahua succumb to obesity.

The older Chihuahua will need more supervision if his eyesight and hearing are diminished.

When the Time Has Come

There is going to come a time when your dog has reached an advanced age and is in severe and constant pain, or has an illness that cannot be cured. The time has now come to say good-bye and to have your beloved pet humanely euthanized by your veterinarian.

With consistent care and loving attention, your Chihuahua will give you playful companionship for many years.

This will most likely cause you great emotional pain, but when your pet has reached this stage, it is much better for you and your pet to take the appropriate action. This author has gone through this many times in thirty-five years and so is readily attuned to your emotional attachments to your friend and companion of many years.

As difficult as it will be, you should not leave the dog at the animal hospital and walk away. Take a friend with you to help you cope. Although it will be a great burden on you emotionally, it is recommended that you hold the dog in your arms, comforting him with soothing vocal sounds while the anesthetic is being administered. It will be a loving and humane farewell to your faithful friend. Make the arrangements in advance, and take care of all office requirements before the scheduled time. Then when the procedure has been completed, you will be able to walk out of the office

without looking back. Yes, you will shed many a tear for some time to come, but you will also have many fond memories of the wonderful times you have had with your Chihuahua.

There will come a time when you will be able to tell some great stories about all the things that your Chihuahua could do. How she understood your every word. How she comforted you in times of sadness. How she brought great joy to your life. No one can take those wonderful memories away from you.

Should you get another Chihuahua? Of course, but not right away. Take a little time for the hurt to fade away. You will know when the time is right to get another Chihuahua. Do not try to replace the Chihuahua that you have lost, and above all do not compare the new puppy with the old one. Each Chihuahua is an individual in his own right. Each will provide you with many years of love and companionship, but each will do it in his own way. Give your new Chihuahua a chance to be himself and not a clone of the one you have lost. Enjoy your new Chihuahua!

Your Happy, Healthy Pet

Your Dog's Name ______________________________

Name on Your Dog's Pedigree (if your dog has one) ______________________________

____

Where Your Dog Came From ______________________________

____

Your Dog's Birthday ______________________________

Your Dog's Veterinarian

Name ______________________________

Address ______________________________

Phone Number ______________________________

Emergency Number ______________________________

Your Dog's Health

Vaccines

type ______________________ date given __________

type ______________________ date given __________

type ______________________ date given __________

type ______________________ date given __________

Heartworm

date tested __________ type used ______________ start date __________

Your Dog's License Number ______________________________

Groomer's Name and Number ______________________________

Dogsitter/Walker's Name and Number ______________________________

Awards Your Dog Has Won

Award ______________________ date earned __________

Award ______________________ date earned __________

part three

Enjoying your Dog

chapter 8

Basic Training

by Ian Dunbar, Ph.D., MRCVS

Training is the jewel in the crown—the most important aspect of doggy husbandry. There is no more important variable influencing dog behavior and temperament than the dog's education: A well-trained, well-behaved and good-natured puppydog is always a joy to live with, but an untrained and uncivilized dog can be a perpetual nightmare. Moreover, deny the dog an education and it will not have the opportunity to fulfill its own canine potential; neither will it have the ability to communicate effectively with its human companions.

Luckily, modern psychological training methods are easy, efficient and effective and, above all, considerably dog-friendly and user-friendly. Doggy education is as simple as it is enjoyable. But before you can have a good time play-training with your new dog, you have to learn what to do and how to do it. There is no bigger variable influencing the success of dog training than the *owner's* experience and expertise. *Before you embark on the dog's education, you must first educate yourself.*

Basic Training for Owners

Ideally, basic owner training should begin well *before* you select your dog. Find out all you can about your chosen breed first, then master rudimentary training and handling skills. If you already have your puppy/dog, owner training is a dire emergency—the clock is running! Especially for puppies, the first few weeks at home are the most important and influential days in the dog's life. Indeed, the cause of most adolescent and adult problems may be traced back to the initial days the pup explores his new home. This is the time to establish the *status quo*—to teach the puppy/dog how you would like him to behave and so prevent otherwise quite predictable problems.

In addition to consulting breeders and breed books such as this one (which understandably have a positive breed bias), seek out as many pet owners with your breed you can find. Good points are obvious. What you want to find out are the breed-specific *problems,* so you can nip them in the bud. In particular, you should talk to owners with *adolescent* dogs and make a list of all anticipated problems. Most important, *test drive* at least half a dozen adolescent and adult dogs of your breed yourself. An eight-week-old puppy is deceptively easy to handle, but she will acquire adult size, speed and strength in just four months, so you should learn now what to prepare for.

Puppy and pet dog training classes offer a convenient venue to locate pet owners and observe dogs in action. For a list of suitable trainers in your area, contact the Association of Pet Dog Trainers (see Chapter 13). You may also begin your basic owner training by observing other owners in class. Watch as many classes and test

drive as many dogs as possible. Select an upbeat, dog-friendly, people-friendly, fun-and-games, puppydog pet training class to learn the ropes. Also, watch training videos and read training books (see Chapter 12). You must find out what to do and how to do it *before* you have to do it.

Principles of Training

Most people think training comprises teaching the dog to do things such as sit, speak and roll over, but even a four-week-old pup knows how to do these things already. Instead, the first step in training involves teaching the dog human words for each dog behavior and activity and for each aspect of the dog's environment. That way you, the owner, can more easily participate in the dog's domestic education by directing him to perform specific actions appropriately, that is, at the right time, in the right place, and so on. Training opens communication channels, enabling an educated dog to at least understand the owner's requests.

In addition to teaching a dog *what* we want her to do, it is also necessary to teach her *why* she should do what we ask. Indeed, 95 percent of training revolves around motivating the dog *to want to do* what we want. Dogs often understand what their owners want; they just don't see the point of doing it—especially when the owner's repetitively boring and seemingly senseless instructions are totally at odds with much more pressing and exciting doggy distractions. It is not so much the dog who is being stubborn or dominant; rather, it is the owner who has failed to acknowledge the dog's needs and feelings and to approach training from the dog's point of view.

The Meaning of Instructions

The secret to successful training is learning how to use training lures to predict or prompt specific behaviors—to coax the dog to do what you want *when* you want. Any highly valued object (such as a treat or toy) may be used as a lure, which the dog will follow with his eyes and nose. Moving the lure in specific ways entices the dog to move his nose, head and entire body in specific ways. In fact, by learning the art of manipulating various lures, it is possible to teach the dog to assume virtually any body position and perform any action. Once you have control over the expression of the dog's behaviors and can elicit any body position or behavior at will, you can easily teach the dog to perform on request.

Tell your dog what you want him to do, use a lure to entice him to respond correctly, then profusely praise

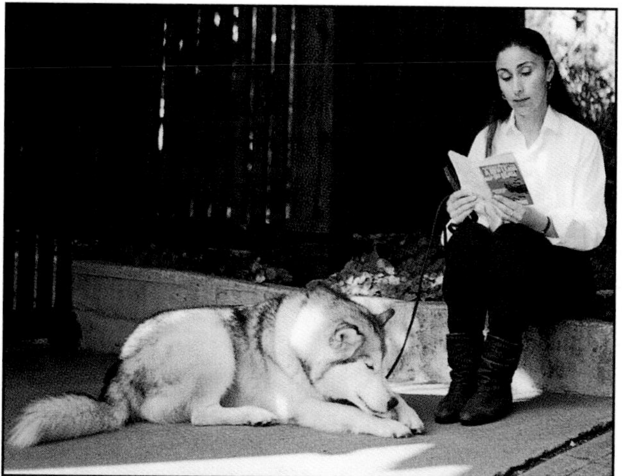

Teach your dog words for each activity he needs to know, like down.

and maybe reward him once he performs the desired action. For example, verbally request "Fido, sit!" while you move a squeaky toy upwards and backwards over the dog's muzzle (lure-movement and hand signal), smile knowingly as he looks up (to follow the lure) and sits down (as a result of canine anatomical engineering), then praise him to distraction ("Gooood Fido!"). Squeak the toy, offer a training treat and give your dog and yourself a pat on the back.

Being able to elicit desired responses over and over enables the owner to reward the dog over and over. Consequently, the dog begins to think training is fun. For example, the more the dog is rewarded for sitting, the more she enjoys sitting. Eventually the dog comes

to realize that, whereas most sitting is appreciated, sitting immediately upon request usually prompts especially enthusiastic praise and a slew of high-level rewards. The dog begins to sit on cue much of the time, showing that she is starting to grasp the meaning of the owner's verbal request and hand signal.

Why Comply?

Most dogs enjoy initial lure/reward training and are only too happy to comply with their owners' wishes. Unfortunately, repetitive drilling without appreciative feedback tends to diminish the dog's enthusiasm until he eventually fails to see the point of complying anymore. Moreover, as the dog approaches adolescence he becomes more easily distracted as he develops other interests. Lengthy sessions with repetitive exercises tend to bore and demotivate both parties. If it's not fun, the owner doesn't do it and neither does the dog.

Integrate training into your dog's life: The greater number of training sessions each day and the *shorter* they are, the more willingly compliant your dog will become. Make sure to have a short (just a few seconds) training interlude before every enjoyable canine activity. For example, ask your dog to sit to greet people, to sit before you throw his Frisbee, and to sit for his supper. Really, sitting is no different from a canine "please." Also, include numerous short training interludes during every enjoyable canine pastime, for example, when playing with the dog or when he is running in the park. In this fashion, doggy distractions may be effectively converted into rewards for training. Just as all games have rules, fun becomes training . . . and training becomes fun.

Eventually, rewards actually become unnecessary to continue motivating your dog. If trained with consideration and kindness, performing the desired behaviors will become self-rewarding and, in a sense, your dog will motivate himself. Just as it is not necessary to reward a human companion during an enjoyable walk in the park, or following a game of tennis, it is hardly necessary to reward our best friend—the dog—for walking by our side or while playing fetch. Human company during enjoyable activities is reward enough for most dogs.

To train your dog, you need gentle hands, a loving heart and a good attitude.

Even though your dog has become self-motivating, it's still good to praise and pet him a lot and offer rewards once in a while, especially for a good job well done. And if for no other reason, praising and rewarding others is good for the human heart.

Punishment

Without a doubt, lure/reward training is by far the best way to teach: Entice your dog to do what you want and then reward him for doing so. Unfortunately, a human shortcoming is to take the good for granted and to moan and groan at the bad. Specifically, the dog's many good behaviors are ignored while the owner focuses on punishing the dog for making mistakes. In extreme cases, instruction is *limited* to punishing mistakes made by a trainee dog, child, employee or husband, even though it has been proven punishment training is notoriously inefficient and ineffective and is decidedly unfriendly and combative. It teaches the dog that training is a drag, almost as quickly as it teaches the dog to dislike his trainer. Why treat our best friends like our worst enemies?

Punishment training is also much more laborious and time consuming. Whereas it takes only a finite amount of time to teach a dog what to chew, for example, it takes much, much longer to punish the dog for each and every mistake. Remember, *there is only one right way!* So why not teach that right way from the outset?!

To make matters worse, punishment training causes severe lapses in the dog's reliability. Since it is obviously impossible to punish the dog each and every time she misbehaves, the dog quickly learns to distinguish between those times when she must comply (so as to avoid impending punishment) and those times when she need not comply, because punishment is impossible. Such times include when the dog is off leash and only six feet away, when the owner is otherwise engaged (talking to a friend, watching television, taking a shower, tending to the baby or chatting on the telephone), or when the dog is left at home alone.

Instances of misbehavior will be numerous when the owner is away, because even when the dog complied in the owner's looming presence, he did so unwillingly. The dog was forced to act against his will, rather than moulding his will to want to please. Hence, when the owner is absent, not only does the dog know he need not comply, he simply does not want to. Again, the trainee is not a stubborn vindictive beast, but rather the trainer has failed to teach.

Punishment training invariably creates unpredictable Jekyll and Hyde behavior.

Trainer's Tools

Many training books extol the virtues of a vast array of training paraphernalia and electronic and metallic gizmos, most of which are designed for canine restraint, correction and punishment, rather than for actual facilitation of doggy education. In reality, most effective training tools are not found in stores; they come from within ourselves. In addition to a willing dog, all you really need is a functional human brain, gentle hands, a loving heart and a good attitude.

In terms of equipment, all dogs do require a quality buckle collar to sport dog tags and to attach the leash (for safety and to comply with local leash laws). Hollow chewtoys (like Kongs or sterilized longbones) and a dog bed or collapsible crate are a must for housetraining. Three additional tools are required:

1. specific lures (training treats and toys) to predict and prompt specific desired behaviors;
2. rewards (praise, affection, training treats and toys) to reinforce for the dog what a lot of fun it all is; and
3. knowledge—how to convert the dog's favorite activities and games (potential distractions to training) into "life-rewards," which may be employed to facilitate training.

The most powerful of these is *knowledge*. Education is the key! Watch training classes, participate in training classes, watch videos, read books, enjoy playtraining with your dog, and then your dog will say "Please," and your dog will say "Thank you!"

Housetraining

If dogs were left to their own devices, certainly they would chew, dig and bark for entertainment and then no doubt highlight a few areas of their living space with sprinkles of urine, in much the same way we decorate by hanging pictures. Consequently, when we ask a dog to live with us, we must teach him *where* he may dig and perform his toilet duties, *what* he may chew and *when* he may bark. After all, when left at home alone for many hours, we cannot expect the dog to amuse himself by completing crosswords or watching the soaps on TV!

Also, it would be decidedly unfair to keep the house rules a secret from the dog, and then get angry and punish the poor critter for inevitably transgressing rules he did not even know existed. Remember, without adequate education and guidance, the dog will be forced to establish his own rules—doggy rules—that most probably will be at odds with the owner's view of domestic living.

Since most problems develop during the first few days the dog is at home, prospective dog owners must be certain they are quite clear about the principles of housetraining *before* they get a dog. Early misbehaviors quickly become established as the status quo—

becoming firmly entrenched as hard-to-break bad habits, which set the precedent for years to come. Make sure to teach your dog good habits right from the start. Good habits are just as hard to break as bad ones!

Ideally, when a new dog comes home, try to arrange for someone to be present for as much as possible during the first few days (for adult dogs) or weeks for puppies. With only a little forethought, it is surprisingly easy to find a puppy sitter, such as a retired person, who would be willing to eat from your refrigerator and watch your television while keeping an eye on the newcomer to encourage the dog to play with chewtoys and to ensure he goes outside on a regular basis.

Potty Training

To teach the dog where to relieve himself:

1. never let him make a single mistake;
2. let him know where you want him to go; and
3. handsomely reward him for doing so: "GOOOOOOOD DOG!!!" liver treat, liver treat, liver treat!

Preventing Mistakes

A single mistake is a training disaster, since it heralds many more in future weeks. And each time the dog soils the house, this further reinforces the dog's unfortunate preference for an indoor, carpeted toilet. *Do not let an unhousetrained dog have full run of the house if you are away from home or cannot pay full attention.* Instead, confine the dog to an area where elimination is appropriate, such as an outdoor run or, better still, a small, comfortable indoor kennel with access to an outdoor run. When confined in this manner, most dogs will naturally housetrain themselves.

If that's not possible, confine the dog to an area, such as a utility room, kitchen, basement or garage, where elimination may not be desired in the long run but as an interim measure it is certainly preferable to doing it all around the house. Use newspaper to cover the floor of the dog's day room. The newspaper may be used to soak up the urine and to wrap up and dispose of the feces. Once your dog develops a preferred spot for eliminating, it is only necessary to cover that part of the floor with newspaper. The smaller papered area may then be moved (only a little each day) towards the door to the outside. Thus the dog will develop the tendency to go to the door when he needs to relieve himself.

The first few weeks at home are the most important and influential in your dog's life.

Never confine an unhousetrained dog to a crate for long periods. Doing so would force the dog to soil the crate and ruin its usefulness as an aid for housetraining (see the following discussion).

Teaching Where

In order to teach your dog where you would like her to do her business, you have to be there to direct the proceedings—an obvious, yet often neglected, fact of life. In order to be there to teach the dog *where* to go, you need to know *when* she needs to go. Indeed, the success of housetraining depends on the owner's ability to predict these times. Certainly, a regular feeding schedule will facilitate prediction somewhat, but there is nothing like "loading the deck" and influencing the timing of the outcome yourself!

Whenever you are at home, make sure the dog is under constant supervision and/or confined to a small

area. If already well trained, simply instruct the dog to lie down in his bed or basket. Alternatively, confine the dog to a crate (doggy den) or tie-down (a short, 18-inch lead that can be clipped to an eye hook in the baseboard). Short-term close confinement strongly inhibits urination and defecation, since the dog does not want to soil his sleeping area. Thus, when you release the puppydog each hour, he will definitely need to urinate immediately and defecate every third or fourth hour. Keep the dog confined to his doggy den and take him to his intended toilet area each hour, every hour, and on the hour.

When taking your dog outside, instruct him to sit quietly before opening the door—he will soon learn to sit by the door when he needs to go out!

Teaching Why

Being able to predict when the dog needs to go enables the owner to be on the spot to praise and reward the dog. Each hour, hurry the dog to the intended toilet area in the yard, issue the appropriate instruction ("Go pee!" or "Go poop!"), then give the dog three to four minutes to produce. Praise and offer a couple of training treats when successful. The treats are important because many people fail to praise their dogs with feeling . . . and housetraining is hardly the time for understatement. So either loosen up and enthusiastically praise that dog: "Wuzzzer-wuzzer-wuzzer, hoooser good wuffer den? Hoooo went pee for Daddy?" Or say "Good dog!" as best you can and offer the treats for effect.

Following elimination is an ideal time for a spot of playtraining in the yard or house. Also, an empty dog may be allowed greater freedom around the house for the next half hour or so, just as long as you keep an eye out to make sure he does not get into other kinds of mischief. If you are preoccupied and cannot pay full attention, confine the dog to his doggy den once more to enjoy a peaceful snooze or to play with his many chewtoys.

If your dog does not eliminate within the allotted time outside—no biggie! Back to his doggy den, and then try again after another hour.

As I own large dogs, I always feel more relaxed walking an empty dog, knowing that I will not need to finish our stroll weighted down with bags of feces! Beware of falling into the trap of walking the dog to get it to eliminate. The good ol' dog walk is such an enormous highlight in the dog's life that it represents the single biggest potential reward in domestic dogdom. However, when in a hurry, or during inclement weather, many owners abruptly terminate the walk the moment the dog has done its business. This, in effect, severely punishes the dog for doing the right thing, in the right place at the right time. Consequently, many dogs become strongly inhibited from eliminating outdoors because they know it will signal an abrupt end to an otherwise thoroughly enjoyable walk.

Instead, instruct the dog to relieve himself in the yard prior to going for a walk. If you follow the above instructions, most dogs soon learn to eliminate on cue. As soon as the dog eliminates, praise (and offer a treat or two)—"Good dog! Let's go walkies!" Use the walk as a reward for eliminating in the yard. If the dog does not go, put him back in his doggy den and think about a walk later on. You will find with a "No feces–no walk" policy, your dog will become one of the fastest defecators in the business.

If you do not have a back yard, instruct the dog to eliminate right outside your front door prior to the walk. Not only will this facilitate clean up and disposal of the feces in your own trash can but, also, the walk may again be used as a colossal reward.

Chewing and Barking

Short-term close confinement also teaches the dog that occasional quiet moments are a reality of domestic living. Your puppydog is extremely impressionable during his first few weeks at home. Regular

confinement at this time soon exerts a calming influence over the dog's personality. Remember, once the dog is housetrained and calmer, there will be a whole lifetime ahead for the dog to enjoy full run of the house and garden. On the other hand, by letting the newcomer have unrestricted access to the entire household and allowing him to run willy-nilly, he will most certainly develop a bunch of behavior problems in short order, no doubt necessitating confinement later in life. It would not be fair to remedially restrain and confine a dog you have trained, through neglect, to run free.

When confining the dog, make sure he always has an impressive array of suitable chewtoys. Kongs and sterilized longbones (both readily available from pet stores) make the best chewtoys, since they are hollow and may be stuffed with treats to heighten the dog's interest. For example, by stuffing the little hole at the top of a Kong with a small piece of freeze-dried liver, the dog will not want to leave it alone.

Remember, treats do not have to be junk food and they certainly should not represent extra calories. Rather, treats should be part of each dog's regular daily diet: Some food may be served in the dog's bowl for breakfast and dinner, some food may be used as training treats, and some food may be used for stuffing chewtoys. I regularly stuff my dogs' many Kongs with different shaped biscuits and kibble. The kibble seems to fall out fairly easily, as do the oval-shaped biscuits, thus rewarding the dog instantaneously for checking out the chewtoys. The bone-shaped biscuits fall out after a while, rewarding the dog for worrying at the chewtoy. But the triangular biscuits never come out. They remain inside the Kong as lures,

Make sure your puppy has suitable chewtoys.

maintaining the dog's fascination with its chewtoy. To further focus the dog's interest, I always make sure to flavor the triangular biscuits by rubbing them with a little cheese or freeze-dried liver.

If stuffed chewtoys are reserved especially for times the dog is confined, the puppydog will soon learn to enjoy quiet moments in her doggy den and she will quickly develop a chewtoy habit—a good habit! This is a simple *passive training* process; all the owner has to do is set up the situation and the dog all but trains herself—easy and effective. Even when the dog is given run of the house, her first inclination will be to indulge her rewarding chewtoy habit rather than destroying less-attractive household articles, such as curtains, carpets, chairs and compact disks. Similarly, a chewtoy chewer will be less inclined to scratch and chew herself excessively. Also, if the dog busies herself as a recreational chewer, she will be less inclined to develop into a recreational barker or digger when left at home alone.

Stuff a number of chewtoys whenever the dog is left confined and remove the extra-special-tasting treats when you return. Your dog will now amuse himself with his chewtoys before falling asleep and then resume playing with his chewtoys when he expects you to return. Since most owner-absent misbehavior happens right after you leave and right before your expected return, your puppydog will now be conveniently preoccupied with his chewtoys at these times.

To teach come, call your dog, open your arms as a welcoming signal, wave a toy or a treat and praise for every step in your direction.

Come and Sit

Most puppies will happily approach virtually anyone, whether called or not; that is, until they collide with

adolescence and develop other more important doggy interests, such as sniffing a multiplicity of exquisite odors on the grass. Your mission, Mr. and/or Ms. Owner, is to teach and reward the pup for coming reliably, willingly and happily when called—and you have just three months to get it done. Unless adequately reinforced, your puppy's tendency to approach people will self-destruct by adolescence.

Call your dog ("Fido, come!"), open your arms (and maybe squat down) as a welcoming signal, waggle a treat or toy as a lure, and reward the puppydog when he comes running. Do not wait to praise the dog until he reaches you—he may come 95 percent of the way and then run off after some distraction. Instead, praise the dog's *first* step towards you and continue praising enthusiastically for *every* step he takes in your direction.

When the rapidly approaching puppy dog is three lengths away from impact, instruct him to sit ("Fido, sit!") and hold the lure in front of you in an outstretched hand to prevent him from hitting you midchest and knocking you flat on your back! As Fido decelerates to nose the lure, move the treat upwards and backwards just over his muzzle with an upwards motion of your extended arm (palm-upwards). As the dog looks up to follow the lure, he will sit down (if he jumps up, you are holding the lure too high). Praise the dog for sitting. Move backwards and call him again. Repeat this many times over, always praising when Fido comes and sits; on occasion, reward him.

For the first couple of trials, use a training treat both as a lure to entice the dog to come and sit and as a reward for doing so. Thereafter, try to use different items as lures and rewards. For example, lure the dog with a Kong or Frisbee but reward her with a food treat. Or lure the dog with a food treat but pat her and throw a tennis ball as a reward. After just a few repetitions, dispense with the lures and rewards; the dog will begin to respond willingly to your verbal requests and hand signals just for the prospect of praise from your heart and affection from your hands.

Instruct every family member, friend and visitor how to get the dog to come and sit. Invite people over for a series of pooch parties; do not keep the pup a secret—let other people enjoy this puppy, and let the pup enjoy other people. Puppydog parties are not only fun, they easily attract a lot of people to help *you* train *your* dog. Unless you teach your dog *how* to meet people, that is, to sit for greetings, no doubt the dog will resort to jumping up. Then you and the visitors will get annoyed, and the dog will be punished. This is not fair. *Send out those invitations for puppy parties and teach your dog to be mannerly and socially acceptable.*

Even though your dog quickly masters obedient recalls in the house, his reliability may falter when playing in the back yard or local park. Ironically, it is *the owner* who has unintentionally trained the dog *not* to respond in these instances. By allowing the dog to play and run around and otherwise have a good time, but then to call the dog to put him on leash to take him home, the dog quickly learns playing is fun but training is a drag. Thus, playing in the park becomes a severe distraction, which works against training. Bad news!

Instead, whether playing with the dog off leash or on leash, request him to come at frequent intervals—say, every minute or so. On most occasions, praise and pet the dog for a few seconds while he is sitting, then tell him to go play again. For especially fast recalls, offer a couple of training treats and take the time to praise and pet the dog enthusiastically before releasing him. The dog will learn that coming when called is not necessarily the end of the play session, and neither is it the end of the world; rather, it signals an enjoyable, quality time-out with the owner before resuming play once more. In fact, playing in the park now becomes a very effective life-reward, which works to facilitate training by reinforcing each obedient and timely recall. Good news!

Sit, Down, Stand and Rollover

Teaching the dog a variety of body positions is easy for owner and dog, impressive for spectators and

extremely useful for all. Using lure-reward techniques, it is possible to train several positions at once to verbal commands or hand signals (which impress the socks off onlookers).

Sit and ***down***—the two control commands—prevent or resolve nearly a hundred behavior problems. For example, if the dog happily and obediently sits or lies down when requested, he cannot jump on visitors, dash out the front door, run around and chase its tail, pester other dogs, harass cats or annoy family, friends or strangers. Additionally, "sit" or "down" are better emergency commands for off-leash control.

It is easier to teach and maintain a reliable sit than maintain a reliable recall. *Sit* is the purest and simplest of commands—either the dog is sitting or he is not. If there is any change of circumstances or potential danger in the park, for example, simply instruct the dog to sit. If he sits, you have a number of options: allow the dog to resume playing when he is safe; walk up and put the dog on leash, or call the dog. The dog will be much more likely to come when called if he has already acknowledged his compliance by sitting. If the dog does not sit in the park—train him to!

Stand and ***rollover-stay*** are the two positions for examining the dog. Your veterinarian will love you to distraction if you take a little time to teach the dog to stand still and roll over and play possum. Also, your vet bills will be smaller. The rollover-stay is an especially useful command and is really just a variation of the down-stay: whereas the dog lies prone in the traditional down, she lies supine in the rollover-stay.

As with teaching come and sit, the training techniques to teach the dog to assume all other body positions on cue are user-friendly and dog-friendly. Simply give the appropriate request, lure the dog into the desired body position using a training treat or toy and then *praise* (and maybe reward) the dog as soon as he complies. Try not to touch the dog to get him to respond. If you teach the dog by guiding him into position, the dog will quickly learn that rump-pressure means sit, for example, but as yet you still have no control over your dog if he is just six feet away. It will still be necessary to teach the dog to sit on request. So do not make training a time-consuming two-step process; instead, teach the dog to sit to a verbal request or hand signal from the outset. Once the dog sits willingly when requested, by all means use your hands to pet the dog when he does so.

To teach ***down*** when the dog is already sitting, say "Fido, down!," hold the lure in one hand (palm down) and lower that hand to the floor between the dog's forepaws. As the dog lowers his head to follow the lure, slowly move the lure away from the dog just a fraction (in front of his paws). The dog will lie down as he stretches his nose forward to follow the lure. Praise the dog when he does so. If the dog stands up, you pulled the lure away too far and too quickly.

When teaching the dog to lie down from the standing position, say "down" and lower the lure to the floor as before. Once the dog has lowered his forequarters and assumed a play bow, gently and slowly move the lure *towards* the dog between his forelegs. Praise the dog as soon as his rear end plops down.

After just a couple of trials it will be possible to alternate sits and downs and have the dog energetically perform doggy push-ups. Praise the dog a lot, and after half a dozen or so push-ups reward the dog with a training treat or toy. You will notice the more energetically you move your arm—upwards (palm up) to get the dog to sit, and downwards (palm down) to get the dog to lie down—the more energetically the dog responds to your requests. Now try training the dog in silence and you will notice he has also learned to respond to hand signals. Yeah! Not too shabby for the first session.

To teach ***stand*** from the sitting position, say "Fido, stand," slowly move the lure half a dog-length away from the dog's nose, keeping it at nose level, and praise the dog as he stands to follow the lure. As soon

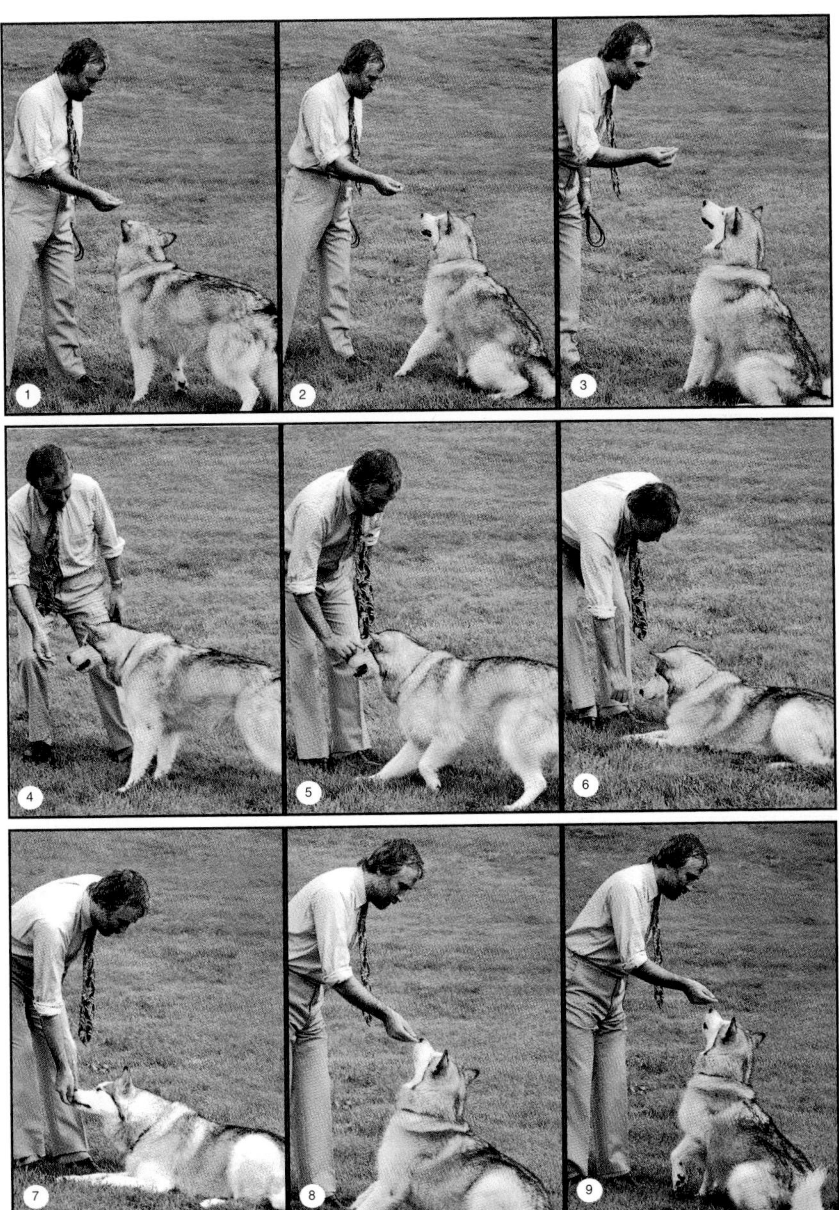

Using a food lure to teach sit, down and stand. 1) "Phoenix, Sit." 2) Hand palm upwards, move lure up and back over dog's muzzle. 3) "Good sit, Phoenix!" 4) "Phoenix, down." 5) Hand palm downwards, move lure down to lie between dog's forepaws. 6) "Phoenix, off. Good down, Phoenix!" 7) "Phoenix, sit!" 8) Palm upwards, move lure up and back, keeping it close to dog's muzzle. 9) "Good sit, Phoenix!"

10) "Phoenix, stand!" 11) Move lure away from dog at nose height, then lower it a tad. 12) "Phoenix, off! Good stand, Phoenix!" 13) "Phoenix, down!" 14) Hand palm downwards, move lure down to lie between dog's forepaws. 15) "Phoenix, off! Good down-stay, Phoenix!" 16) "Phoenix, stand!" 17) Move lure away from dog's muzzle up to nose height. 18) "Phoenix, off! Good stand-stay, Phoenix. Now we'll make the vet and groomer happy!"

as the dog stands, lower the lure to just beneath the dog's chin to entice him to look down; otherwise he will stand and then sit immediately. To prompt the dog to stand from the down position, move the lure half a dog-length upwards and away from the dog, holding the lure at standing nose height from the floor.

Teaching ***rollover*** is best started from the down position, with the dog lying on one side, or at least with both hind legs stretched out on the same side. Say "Fido, bang!" and move the lure backwards and alongside the dog's muzzle to its elbow (on the side of its outstretched hind legs). Once the dog looks to the side and backwards, very slowly move the lure upwards to the dog's shoulder and backbone. Tickling the dog in the goolies (groin area) often invokes a reflex-raising of the hind leg as an appeasement gesture, which facilitates the tendency to roll over. If you move the lure too quickly and the dog jumps into the standing position, have patience and start again. As soon as the dog rolls onto its back, keep the lure stationary and mesmerize the dog with a relaxing tummy rub.

To teach ***rollover-stay*** when the dog is standing or moving, say "Fido, bang!" and give the appropriate hand signal (with index finger pointed and thumb cocked in true Sam Spade fashion), then in one fluid movement lure him to first lie down and then rollover-stay as above.

Teaching the dog to ***stay*** in each of the above four positions becomes a piece of cake after first teaching the dog not to worry at the toy or treat training lure. This is best accomplished by hand feeding dinner kibble. Hold a piece of kibble firmly in your hand and softly instruct "Off!" Ignore any licking and slobbering *for however long the dog worries at the treat*, but say "Take it!" and offer the kibble *the instant* the dog breaks contact with his muzzle. Repeat this a few times, and then up the ante and insist the dog remove his muzzle for one whole second before offering the kibble. Then progressively refine your criteria and have the dog not touch your hand (or treat) for longer and longer periods on each trial, such as for two seconds, four seconds, then six, ten, fifteen, twenty, thirty seconds and so on. The dog soon learns: (1) worrying at the treat never gets results, whereas (2) noncontact is often rewarded after a variable time lapse.

Teaching ***"Off!"*** has many useful applications in its own right. Additionally, instructing the dog not to touch a training lure often produces spontaneous and magical stays. Request the dog to stand-stay, for example, and not to touch the lure. At first set your sights on a short two-second stay before rewarding the dog. (Remember, every long journey begins with a single step.) However, on subsequent trials, gradually and progressively increase the length of stay required to receive a reward. In no time at all your dog will stand calmly for a minute or so.

Relevancy Training

Once you have taught the dog what you expect her to do when requested to come, sit, lie down, stand, rollover and stay, the time is right to teach the dog *why* she should comply with your wishes. The secret is to have many (*many*) extremely short training interludes (two to five seconds each) at numerous (*numerous*) times during the course of the dog's day. Especially work with the dog immediately *before* the dog's good times and *during* the dog's good times. For example, ask your dog to sit and/or lie down each time before opening doors, serving meals, offering treats and tummy rubs; ask the dog to perform a few controlled doggy push-ups before letting her off-leash or throwing a tennis ball; and perhaps request the dog to sit-down-sit-stand-down-stand-rollover before inviting her to cuddle on the couch.

Similarly, request the dog to sit many times during play or on walks, and in no time at all the dog will be only too pleased to follow your instructions because he has learned that a compliant response heralds all sorts of goodies. Basically all you are trying to teach the dog is how to say please: "Please throw the tennis ball. Please may I snuggle on the couch."

Remember, whereas it is important to keep training interludes short, it is equally important to have many short sessions each and every day. The shortest (and most useful) session comprises asking the dog to sit and then go play during a play session. When trained this way, your dog will soon associate training with good times. In fact, the dog may be unable to distinguish between training and good times and, indeed, there should be no distinction. The warped concept that training involves forcing the dog to comply and/or dominating his will is totally at odds with the picture of a truly well-trained dog. In reality, enjoying a game of training with a dog is no different from enjoying a game of backgammon or tennis with a friend; and walking with a dog should be no different from strolling with buddies on the golf course.

Walk by Your Side

Many people attempt to teach a dog to heel by putting him on a leash and physically correcting the dog when he makes mistakes. There are a number of things seriously wrong with this approach, the first being that most people do not want precision heeling; rather, they simply want the dog to follow or walk by their side. Second, when physically restrained during "training," even though the dog may grudgingly mope by your side when "handcuffed" on leash, let's see what happens when he is off leash. History! The dog is in the next county because he never enjoyed walking with you on leash and you have no control over him off leash. So let's just teach the dog off leash from the outset to *want* to walk with us. Third, if the dog has not been trained to heel, it is a trifle hasty to think about punishing the poor dog for making mistakes and breaking heeling rules he didn't even know existed. This is simply not fair! Surely, if the dog had been adequately taught how to heel, he would seldom make mistakes and hence there would be no need to correct the dog. Remember, each mistake and each correction (punishment) advertise the trainer's inadequacy, not the dog's. The dog is not stubborn, he is not stupid and he is not bad. Even if he were, he would still require training, so let's train him properly.

Let's teach the dog to *enjoy* following us and to *want* to walk by our side offleash. Then it will be easier to teach high-precision off-leash heeling patterns if desired. After attaching the leash for safety on outdoor walks, but before going anywhere, it is necessary to teach the dog specifically not to pull. Now it will be much easier to teach on-leash walking and heeling because the dog already wants to walk with you, he is familiar with the desired walking and heeling positions and he knows not to pull.

Following

Start by training your dog to follow you. Many puppies will follow if you simply walk away from them and maybe click your fingers or chuckle. Adult dogs may require additional enticement to stimulate them to follow, such as a training lure or, at the very least, a lively trainer. To teach the dog to follow: (1) keep walking and (2) walk away from the dog. If the dog attempts to lead or lag, change pace; slow down if the dog forges too far ahead, but speed up if he lags too far behind. Say "Steady!" or "Easy!" each time before you slow down and "Quickly!" or "Hustle!" each time before you speed up, and the dog will learn to change pace on cue. If the dog lags or leads too far, or if he wanders right or left, simply walk quickly in the opposite direction and maybe even run away from the dog and hide.

Practicing is a lot of fun; you can set up a course in your home, yard or park to do this. Indoors, entice the dog to follow upstairs, into a bedroom, into the bathroom, downstairs, around the living room couch, zigzagging between dining room chairs and into the kitchen for dinner. Outdoors, get the dog to follow around park benches, trees, shrubs and along walkways and lines in the grass. (For safety outdoors, it is advisable to attach a long line on the dog, but never exert corrective tension on the line.)

Remember, following has a lot to do with attitude—*your* attitude! Most probably your dog will *not* want to follow Mr. Grumpy Troll with the personality of wilted lettuce. Lighten up—walk with a jaunty step, whistle a happy tune, sing, skip and tell jokes to your dog and he will be right there by your side.

By Your Side

It is smart to train the dog to walk close on one side or the other—either side will do, your choice. When walking, jogging or cycling, it is generally bad news to have the dog suddenly cut in front of you. In fact, I train my dogs to walk "By my side" and "Other side"—both very useful instructions. It is possible to position the dog fairly accurately by looking to the appropriate side and clicking your fingers or slapping your thigh on that side. A precise positioning may be attained by holding a training lure, such as a chewtoy, tennis ball, or food treat. Stop and stand still several times throughout the walk, just as you would when window shopping or meeting a friend. Use the lure to make sure the dog slows down and stays close whenever you stop.

When teaching the dog to heel, we generally want her to sit in heel position when we stop. Teach heel

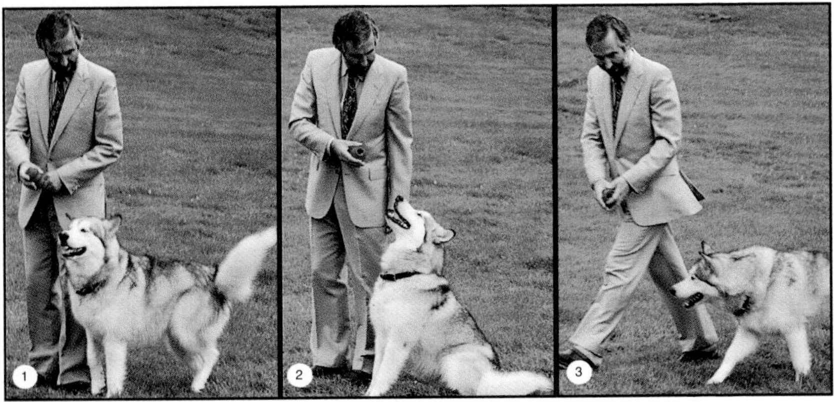

Using a toy to teach sit-heel-sit sequences: 1) "Phoenix, heel!" Standing still, move lure up and back over dog's muzzle.... 2) To position dog sitting in heel position on your left side. 3) "Phoenix, heel!" wagging lure in left hand. Change lure to right hand in preparation for sit signal.

position at the standstill and the dog will learn that the default heel position is sitting by your side (left or right—your choice, unless you wish to compete in obedience trials, in which case the dog must heel on the left).

Several times a day, stand up and call your dog to come and sit in heel position—"Fido, heel!" For example, instruct the dog to come to heel each time there are commercials on TV, or each time you turn a page of a novel, and the dog will get it in a single evening.

Practice straight-line heeling and turns separately. With the dog sitting at heel, teach him to turn in place. After each quarter-turn, half-turn or full turn in place, lure the dog to sit at heel. Now it's time for short straight-line heeling sequences, no more than a few steps at a time. Always think of heeling in terms of Sit-Heel-Sit sequences—start and end with the dog in position and do your best to keep him there when moving. Progressively increase the number of steps in each sequence. When the dog remains close for 20 yards of straight-line heeling, it is time to add a few turns and then sign up for a happy-heeling obedience class to get some advice from the experts.

4) Use hand signal only to lure dog to sit as you stop. Eventually, dog will sit automatically at heel whenever you stop. 5) "Good dog!"

No Pulling on Leash

You can start teaching your dog not to pull on leash anywhere—in front of the television or outdoors—but regardless of location, you must not take a single step with tension in the leash. For a reason known only to dogs, even just a couple of paces of pulling on leash is intrinsically motivating and diabolically rewarding. Instead, attach the leash to the dog's collar, grasp the other end firmly with both hands held close to your chest, and stand still—do not budge an inch. Have somebody watch you with a stopwatch to time your progress, or else you will never believe this will work and so you will not even try the exercise, and your shoulder and the dog's neck will be traumatized for years to come.

Stand still and wait for the dog to stop pulling, and to sit and/or lie down. All dogs stop pulling and sit eventually. Most take only a couple of minutes; the all-time record is 22 ⅕ minutes. Time how long it takes. Gently praise the dog when he stops pulling, and as soon as he sits, enthusiastically praise the dog and take just one step forwards, then immediately stand still. This single step usually demonstrates the ballistic reinforcing nature of pulling on leash; most dogs explode to the end of the leash, so be prepared for the strain. Stand firm and wait for the dog to sit again. Repeat this half a dozen times and you will probably notice a progressive reduction in the force of the dog's one-step explosions and a radical reduction in the time it takes for the dog to sit each time.

As the dog learns "Sit we go" and "Pull we stop," she will begin to walk forward calmly with each single step and automatically sit when you stop. Now try two steps before you stop. Wooooooo! Scary! When the dog has mastered two steps at a time, try for three. After each success, progressively increase the number of steps in the sequence: try four steps and then six, eight, ten and twenty steps before stopping. Congratulations! You are now walking the dog on leash.

Whenever walking with the dog (off leash or on leash), make sure you stop periodically to practice a few position commands and stays before instructing the dog to "Walk on!" (Remember, you want the dog to be compliant everywhere, not just in the kitchen when his dinner is at hand.) For example, stopping every 25 yards to briefly train the dog amounts to over 200 training interludes within a single three-mile stroll. And each training session is in a different location. You will not believe the improvement within just the first mile of the first walk.

To put it another way, integrating training into a walk offers 200 separate opportunities to use the continuance of the walk as a reward to reinforce the dog's education. Moreover, some training interludes may comprise continuing education for the dog's walking skills: Alternate short periods of the dog walking calmly by your side with periods when the dog is allowed to sniff and investigate the environment. Now sniffing odors on the grass and meeting other dogs become rewards which reinforce the dog's calm and mannerly demeanor. Good Lord! Whatever next? Many enjoyable walks together of course. Happy trails!

THE IMPORTANCE OF TRICKS

Nothing will improve a dog's quality of life better than having a few tricks under its belt. Teaching any trick expands the dog's vocabulary, which facilitates communication and improves the owner's control. Also, specific tricks help prevent and resolve specific behavior problems. For example, by teaching the dog to fetch his toys, the dog learns carrying a toy makes the owner happy and, therefore, will be more likely to chew his toy than other inappropriate items.

More important, teaching tricks prompts owners to lighten up and train with a sunny disposition. Really, tricks should be no different from any other behaviors we put on cue. But they are. When teaching tricks, owners have a much sweeter attitude, which in turn motivates the dog and improves her willingness to comply. The dog feels tricks are a blast, but formal commands are a drag. In fact, tricks are so enjoyable, they may be used as rewards in training by asking the dog to come, sit and down-stay and then rollover for a tummy rub. Go on, try it: Crack a smile and even giggle when the dog promptly and willingly lies down and stays.

Most important, performing tricks prompts onlookers to smile and giggle. Many people are scared of dogs, especially large ones. And nothing can be more off-putting for a dog than to be constantly confronted by strangers who don't like him because of his size or the way he looks. Uneasy people put the dog on edge, causing him to back off and bark, only frightening people all the more. And so a vicious circle develops, with the people's fear fueling the dog's fear *and vice versa.* Instead, tie a pink ribbon to your dog's collar and practice all sorts of tricks on walks and in the park, and you will be pleasantly amazed how it changes people's attitudes toward your friendly dog. The dog's repertoire of tricks is limited only by the trainer's imagination. Below I have described three of my favorites:

SPEAK AND SHUSH

The training sequence involved in teaching a dog to bark on request is no different from that used when training any behavior on cue: request—lure—response—reward. As always, the secret of success lies in finding an effective lure. If the dog always barks at the doorbell, for example, say "Rover, speak!", have an accomplice ring the doorbell, then reward the dog for barking. After a few woofs, ask Rover to "Shush!", waggle a food treat under his nose (to entice him to sniff and thus to shush), praise him when quiet and eventually offer the treat as a reward. Alternate "Speak" and "Shush," progressively increasing the length of shush-time between each barking bout.

PLAYBOW

With the dog standing, say "Bow!" and lower the food lure (palm upwards) to rest between the dog's forepaws. Praise as the dog lowers her forequarters and sternum to the ground (as when teaching the down), but then lure the dog to stand and offer the treat. On successive trials, gradually increase the length of time the dog is required to remain in the playbow posture in order to gain a food reward. If the dog's rear end collapses into a down, say nothing and offer no reward; simply start over.

BE A BEAR

With the dog sitting backed into a corner to prevent him from toppling over backwards, say "Be a Bear!" With bent paw and palm down, raise a lure upwards and backwards along the top of the dog's muzzle. Praise the dog when he sits up on his haunches and offer the treat as a reward. To prevent the dog from standing on his hind legs, keep the lure closer to the dog's muzzle. On each trial, progressively increase the length of time the dog is required to sit up to receive a food reward. Since lure/reward training is so easy, teach the dog to stand and walk on his hind legs as well!

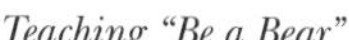

Teaching "Be a Bear"

chapter 9

Getting Active with your Dog

by Bardi McLennan

Once you and your dog have graduated from basic obedience training and are beginning to work together as a team, you can take part in the growing world of dog activities. There are so many fun things to do with your dog! Just remember, people and dogs don't always learn at the same pace, so don't be upset if you (or your dog) need more than two basic training courses before your team becomes operational. Even smart dogs don't go straight to college from kindergarten!

Just as there are events geared to certain types of dogs, so there are ones that are more appealing to certain types of people. In some activities, you give the commands and your dog does the work (upland game hunting is one example), while in others, such as agility, you'll both get a workout. You may want to aim for prestigious titles to add to your dog's name, or you may want nothing more than the sheer enjoyment of being around other people and their dogs. Passive or active, participation has its own rewards.

Consider your dog's physical capabilities when looking into any of the canine activities. It's easy to see that a Basset Hound is not built for the racetrack, nor would a Chihuahua be the breed of choice for pulling a sled. A loyal dog will attempt almost anything you ask him to do, so it is up to you to know your dog's limitations. A dog must be physically sound in order to compete at any level in athletic activities, and being mentally sound is a definite plus. Advanced age, however, may not be a deterrent. Many dogs still hunt and herd at ten or twelve years of age. It's entirely possible for dogs to be "fit at 50." Take your dog for a checkup, explain to your vet the type of activity you have in mind and be guided by his or her findings.

All dogs seem to love playing flyball.

You needn't be restricted to breed-specific sports if it's only fun you're after. Certain AKC activities are limited to designated breeds; however, as each new trial, test or sport has grown in popularity, so has the variety of breeds encouraged to participate at a fun level.

But don't shortchange your fun, or that of your dog, by thinking only of the basic function of her breed. Once a dog has learned how to learn, she can be taught to do just about anything as long as the size of the dog is right for the job and you both think it is fun and rewarding. In other words, you are a team.

To get involved in any of the activities detailed in this chapter, look for the names and addresses of the organizations that sponsor them in Chapter 13. You can also ask your breeder or a local dog trainer for contacts.

You can compete in obedience trials with a well trained dog.

Official American Kennel Club Activities

The following tests and trials are some of the events sanctioned by the AKC and sponsored by various dog clubs. Your dog's expertise will be rewarded with impressive titles. You can participate just for fun, or be competitive and go for those awards.

Obedience

Training classes begin with pups as young as three months of age in kindergarten puppy training, then advance to pre-novice (all exercises on lead) and go on to novice, which is where you'll start off-lead work. In obedience classes dogs learn to sit, stay, heel and come through a variety of exercises. Once you've got the basics down, you can enter obedience trials and work toward earning your dog's first degree, a C.D. (Companion Dog).

The next level is called "Open," in which jumps and retrieves perk up the dog's interest. Passing grades in competition at this level earn a C.D.X. (Companion Dog Excellent). Beyond that lies the goal of the most ambitious—Utility (U.D. and even U.D.X. or OTCh, an Obedience Champion).

Agility

All dogs can participate in the latest canine sport to have gained worldwide popularity for its fun and excitement, agility. It began in England as a canine version of horse show-jumping, but because dogs are more agile and able to perform on verbal commands, extra feats were added such as climbing, balancing and racing through tunnels or in and out of weave poles. Many of the obstacles (regulation or homemade) can be set up in your own backyard. If the agility bug bites, you could end up in international competition!

For starters, your dog should be obedience trained, even though, in the beginning, the lessons may all be taught on lead. Once the dog understands the commands (and you do, too), it's as easy as guiding the dog over a prescribed course, one obstacle at a time. In competition, the race is against the clock, so wear your running shoes! The dog starts with 200 points and the judge deducts for infractions and misadventures along the way.

All dogs seem to love agility and respond to it as if they were being turned loose in a playground paradise. Your dog's enthusiasm will be contagious; agility turns into great fun for dog and owner.

TITLES AWARDED BY THE AKC

Conformation: Ch. (Champion)

Obedience: CD (Companion Dog); CDX (Companion Dog Excellent); UD (Utility Dog); UDX (Utility Dog Excellent); OTCh. (Obedience Trial Champion)

Field: JH (Junior Hunter); SH (Senior Hunter); MH (Master Hunter); AFCh. (Amateur Field Champion); FCh. (Field Champion)

Lure Coursing: JC (Junior Courser); SC (Senior Courser)

Herding: HT (Herding Tested); PT (Pre-Trial Tested); HS (Herding Started); HI (Herding Intermediate); HX (Herding Excellent); HCh. (Herding Champion)

Tracking: TD (Tracking Dog); TDX (Tracking Dog Excellent)

Agility: NAD (Novice Agility); OAD (Open Agility); ADX (Agility Excellent); MAX (Master Agility)

Earthdog Tests: JE (Junior Earthdog); SE (Senior Earthdog); ME (Master Earthdog)

Canine Good Citizen: CGC

Combination: DC (Dual Champion—Ch. and Fch.); TC (Triple Champion—Ch., Fch., and OTCh.)

Field Trials and Hunting Tests

There are field trials and hunting tests for the sporting breeds—retrievers, spaniels and pointing breeds, and for some hounds—Bassets, Beagles and Dachshunds. Field trials are competitive events that test a dog's ability to perform the functions for which she was bred. Hunting tests, which are open to retrievers,

spaniels and pointing breeds only, are noncompetitive and are a means of judging the dog's ability as well as that of the handler.

Hunting is a very large and complex part of canine sports, and if you own one of the breeds that hunts, the events are a great treat for your dog and you. He gets to do what he was bred for, and you get to work with him and watch him do it. You'll be proud of and amazed at what your dog can do.

Fortunately, the AKC publishes a series of booklets on these events, which outline the rules and regulations and include a glossary of the sometimes complicated terms. The AKC also publishes newsletters for field trialers and hunting test enthusiasts. The United Kennel Club (UKC) also has informative materials for the hunter and his dog.

Retrievers and other sporting breeds get to do what they're bred to in hunting tests.

Herding Tests and Trials

Herding, like hunting, dates back to the first known uses man made of dogs. The interest in herding today is widespread, and if you own a herding breed, you can join in the activity. Herding dogs are tested for their natural skills to keep a flock of ducks, sheep or cattle together. If your dog shows potential, you can start at the testing level, where your dog can earn a title for showing an inherent herding ability. With training you can advance to the trial level, where your dog should be capable of controlling even difficult livestock in diverse situations.

Lure Coursing

The AKC Tests and Trials for Lure Coursing are open to traditional sighthounds—Greyhounds, Whippets,

Borzoi, Salukis, Afghan Hounds, Ibizan Hounds and Scottish Deerhounds—as well as to Basenjis and Rhodesian Ridgebacks. Hounds are judged on overall ability, follow, speed, agility and endurance. This is possibly the most exciting of the trials for spectators, because the speed and agility of the dogs is awesome to watch as they chase the lure (or "course") in heats of two or three dogs at a time.

Tracking

Tracking is another activity in which almost any dog can compete because every dog that sniffs the ground when taken outdoors is, in fact, tracking. The hard part comes when the rules as to what, when and where the dog tracks are determined by a person, not the dog! Tracking tests cover a large area of fields, woods and roads. The tracks are laid hours before the dogs go to work on them, and include "tricks" like cross-tracks and sharp turns. If you're interested in search-and-rescue work, this is the place to start.

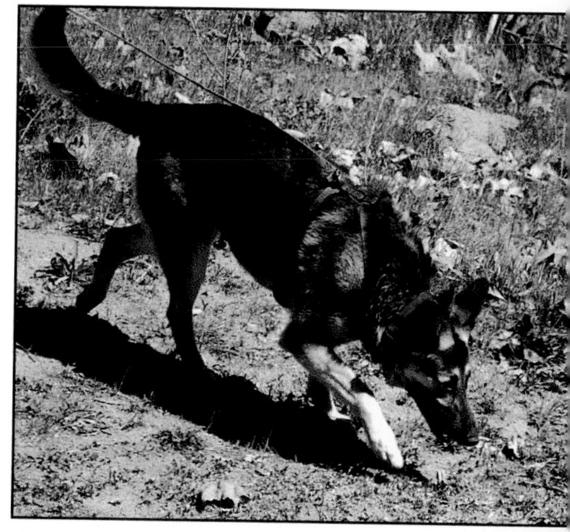

This tracking dog is hot on the trail.

Earthdog Tests for Small Terriers and Dachshunds

These tests are open to Australian, Bedlington, Border, Cairn, Dandie Dinmont, Smooth and Wire Fox, Lakeland, Norfolk, Norwich, Scottish, Sealyham, Skye, Welsh and West Highland White Terriers as well as Dachshunds. The dogs need no prior training for this terrier sport. There is a qualifying test on the day of the event, so dog and handler learn the rules on the spot. These tests, or "digs," sometimes end with informal races in the late afternoon.

Here are some of the extracurricular obedience and racing activities that are not regulated by the AKC or UKC, but are generally run by clubs or a group of dog fanciers and are often open to all.

Canine Freestyle This activity is something new on the scene and is variously likened to dancing, dressage or ice skating. It is meant to show the athleticism of the dog, but also requires showmanship on the part of the dog's handler. If you and your dog like to ham it up for friends, you might want to look into freestyle.

Lure coursing lets sighthounds do what they do best—run!

Scent Hurdle Racing Scent hurdle racing is purely a fun activity sponsored by obedience clubs with members forming competing teams. The height of the hurdles is based on the size of the shortest dog on the team. On a signal, one team dog is released on each of two side-by-side courses and must clear every hurdle before picking up its own dumbbell from a platform and returning over the jumps to the handler. As each dog returns, the next on that team is sent. Of course, that is what the dogs are supposed to do. When the dogs improvise (going under or around the hurdles, stealing another dog's dumbbell, and so forth), it no doubt frustrates the handlers, but just adds to the fun for everyone else.

Flyball This type of racing is similar, but after negotiating the four hurdles, the dog comes to a flyball box, steps on a lever that releases a tennis ball into the air, catches the ball and returns over the hurdles to the starting point. This game also becomes extremely fun for spectators because the dogs sometimes cheat by catching a ball released by the dog in the next lane. Three titles can be earned—Flyball Dog (F.D.), Flyball Dog Excellent (F.D.X.) and Flyball Dog Champion (Fb.D.Ch.)—all awarded by the North American Flyball Association, Inc.

Dogsledding The name conjures up the Rocky Mountains or the frigid North, but you can find dogsled clubs in such unlikely spots as Maryland, North Carolina and Virginia! Dogsledding is primarily for the Nordic breeds such as the Alaskan Malamutes, Siberian Huskies and Samoyeds, but other breeds can try. There are some practical backyard applications to this sport, too. With parental supervision, almost any strong dog could pull a child's sled.

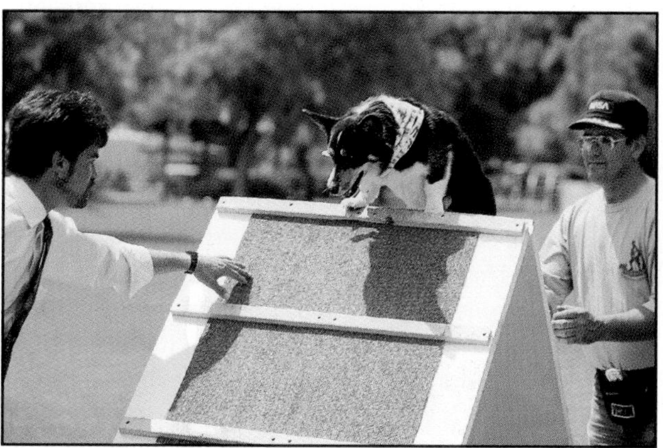

Coming over the A-frame on an agility course.

These are just some of the many recreational ways you can get to know and understand your multifaceted dog better and have fun doing it.

chapter 10

Your Dog and your Family

by Bardi McLennan

Adding a dog automatically increases your family by one, no matter whether you live alone in an apartment or are part of a mother, father and six kids household. The single-person family is fair game for numerous and varied canine misconceptions as to who is dog and who pays the bills, whereas a dog in a houseful of children will consider himself to be just one of the gang, littermates all. One dog and one child may give a dog reason to believe they are both kids or both dogs. Either interpretation requires parental supervision and sometimes speedy intervention.

As soon as one paw goes through the door into your home, Rufus (or Rufina) has to make many adjustments to become a part of your family. Your job is to make him fit in as painlessly as possible. An older dog may have some frame of reference from past experience, but to a 10-week-old puppy, everything is brand new: people, furniture, stairs, when and where people eat, sleep or watch TV, his own place and everyone else's space, smells, sounds, outdoors—everything!

Puppies, and newly acquired dogs of any age, do not need what we think of as "freedom." If you leave a new dog or puppy loose in the house, you will almost certainly return to chaotic destruction and the dog will forever after equate your homecoming with a time of punishment to be dreaded. It is unfair to give your dog what amounts to "freedom to get into trouble." Instead, confine him to a crate for brief periods of your absence (up to three or four hours) and, for the long haul, a workday for example, confine him to one untrashable area with his own toys, a bowl of water and a radio left on (low) in another room.

Lots of pets get along with each other just fine.

For the first few days, when not confined, put Rufus on a long leash tied to your wrist or waist. This umbilical cord method enables the dog to learn all about you from your body language and voice, and to learn by his own actions which things in the house are NO! and which ones are rewarded by "Good dog." Housetraining will be easier with the pup always by your side. Speaking of which, accidents do happen. That goal of "completely housetrained" takes up to a year, or the length of time it takes the pup to mature.

The All-Adult Family

Most dogs in an adults-only household today are likely to be latchkey pets, with no one home all day but the

dog. When you return after a tough day on the job, the dog can and should be your relaxation therapy. But going home can instead be a daily frustration.

Separation anxiety is a very common problem for the dog in a working household. It may begin with whines and barks of loneliness, but it will soon escalate into a frenzied destruction derby. That is why it is so important to set aside the time to teach a dog to relax when left alone in his confined area and to understand that he can trust you to return.

Let the dog get used to your work schedule in easy stages. Confine him to one room and go in and out of that room over and over again. Be casual about it. No physical, voice or eye contact. When the pup no longer even notices your comings and goings, leave the house for varying lengths of time, returning to stay home for a few minutes and gradually increasing the time away. This training can take days, but the dog is learning that you haven't left him forever and that he can trust you.

Any time you leave the dog, but especially during this training period, be casual about your departure. No anxiety-building fond farewells. Just "Bye" and go! Remember the "Good dog" when you return to find everything more or less as you left it.

If things are a mess (or even a disaster) when you return, greet the dog, take him outside to eliminate, and then put him in his crate while you clean up. Rant and rave in the shower! *Do not* punish the dog. You were not there when it happened, and the rule is: Only punish as you catch the dog in the act of wrongdoing. Obviously, it makes sense to get your latchkey puppy when you'll have a week or two to spend on these training essentials.

Family weekend activities should include Rufus whenever possible. Depending on the pup's age, now is the time for a long walk in the park, playtime in the backyard, a hike in the woods. Socializing is as important as health care, good food and physical exercise, so visiting Aunt Emma or Uncle Harry and the next-door neighbor's dog or cat is essential to developing an outgoing, friendly temperament in your pet.

If you are a single adult, socializing Rufus at home and away will prevent him from becoming overly protective of you (or just overly attached) and will also prevent such behavioral problems as dominance or fear of strangers.

Babies

Whether already here or on the way, babies figure larger than life in the eyes of a dog. If the dog is there first, let him in on all your baby preparations in the house. When baby arrives, let Rufus sniff any item of clothing that has been on the baby before Junior comes home. Then let Mom greet the dog first before introducing the new family member. Hold the baby down for the dog to see and sniff, but make sure someone's holding the dog on lead in case of any sudden moves. Don't play keep-away or tease the dog with the baby, which only invites undesirable jumping up.

Dogs are perfect confidants.

The dog and the baby are "family," and for starters can be treated almost as equals. Things rapidly change, however, especially when baby takes to creeping around on all fours on the dog's turf or, better yet, has yummy pudding all over her face and hands! That's when a lot of things in the dog's and baby's lives become more separate than equal.

Toddlers make terrible dog owners, but if you can't avoid the combination, use patient discipline (that is, positive teaching rather than punishment), and use time-outs before you run out of patience.

A dog and a baby (or toddler, or an assertive young child) should never be left alone together. Take the dog with you or confine him. With a baby or youngsters in the house, you'll have plenty of use for that wonderful canine safety device called a crate!

Young Children

Any dog in a house with kids will behave pretty much as the kids do, good or bad. But even good dogs and good children can get into trouble when play becomes rowdy and active.

Teach children how to play nicely with a puppy.

Legs bobbing up and down, shrill voices screeching, a ball hurtling overhead, all add up to exuberant frustration for a dog who's just trying to be part of the gang. In a pack of puppies, any legs or toys being chased would be caught by a set of teeth, and all the pups involved would understand that is how the game is played. Kids do not understand this, nor do parents tolerate it. Bring Rufus indoors before you have reason to regret it. This is time-out, not a punishment.

You can explain the situation to the children and tell them they must play quieter games until the puppy learns not to grab them with his mouth. Unfortunately, you can't explain it that easily to the dog. With adult supervision, they will learn how to play together.

Young children love to tease. Sticking their faces or wiggling their hands or fingers in the dog's face is teasing. To another person it might be just annoying, but it is threatening to a dog. There's another difference: We can make the child stop by an explanation, but the only way a dog can stop it is with a warning growl and then with teeth. Teasing is the major cause of children being bitten by their pets. Treat it seriously.

Older Children

The best age for a child to get a first dog is between the ages of 8 and 12. That's when kids are able to accept some real responsibility for their pet. Even so, take the child's vow of "I will never *ever* forget to feed (brush, walk, etc.) the dog" for what it's worth: a child's good intention at that moment. Most kids today have extra lessons, soccer practice, Little League, ballet, and so forth piled on top of school schedules. There will be many times when Mom will have to come to the dog's rescue. "I walked the dog for you so you can set the table for me" is one way to get around a missed appointment without laying on blame or guilt.

Kids in this age group make excellent obedience trainers because they are into the teaching/learning process themselves and they lack the self-consciousness of adults. Attending a dog show is something the whole family can enjoy, and watching Junior Showmanship may catch the eye of the kids. Older children can begin to get involved in many of the recreational activities that were reviewed in the previous chapter. Some of the agility obstacles, for example, can be set up in the backyard as a family project (with an adult making sure all the equipment is safe and secure for the dog).

Older kids are also beginning to look to the future, and may envision themselves as veterinarians or trainers or show dog handlers or writers of the next Lassie best-seller. Dogs are perfect confidants for these dreams. They won't tell a soul.

Other Pets

Introduce all pets tactfully. In a dog/cat situation, hold the dog, not the cat. Let two dogs meet on neutral turf—a stroll in the park or a walk down the street—with both on loose leads to permit all the normal canine ways of saying hello, including routine sniffing, circling, more sniffing, and so on. Small creatures such as hamsters, chinchillas or mice must be kept safe from their natural predators (dogs and cats).

Festive Family Occasions

Parties are great for people, but not necessarily for puppies. Until all the guests have arrived, put the dog in his crate or in a room where he won't be disturbed. A socialized dog can join the fun later as long as he's not underfoot, annoying guests or into the hors d'oeuvres.

There are a few dangers to consider, too. Doors opening and closing can allow a puppy to slip out unnoticed in the confusion, and you'll be organizing a search party instead of playing host or hostess. Party food and buffet service are not for dogs. Let Rufus party in his crate with a nice big dog biscuit.

At Christmas time, not only are tree decorations dangerous and breakable (and perhaps family heirlooms), but extreme caution should be taken with the lights, cords and outlets for the tree lights and any other festive lighting. Occasionally a dog lifts a leg, ignoring the fact that the tree is indoors. To avoid this, use a canine repellent, made for gardens, on the tree. Or keep him out of the tree room unless supervised. And whatever you do, *don't* invite trouble by hanging his toys on the tree!

Car Travel

Before you plan a vacation by car or RV with Rufus, be sure he enjoys car travel. Nothing spoils a holiday quicker than a carsick dog! Work within the dog's comfort level. Get in the car with the dog in his crate or attached to a canine car safety belt and just sit there until he relaxes. That's all. Next time, get in the car, turn on the engine and go nowhere. Just sit. When that is okay, turn on the engine and go around the block. Now you can go for a ride and include a stop where you get out, leaving the dog for a minute or two.

On a warm day, always park in the shade and leave windows open several inches. And return quickly. It only takes 10 minutes for a car to become an overheated steel death trap.

Motel or Pet Motel?

Not all motels or hotels accept pets, but you have a much better choice today than even a few years ago. To find a dog-friendly lodging, look at *On the Road Again With Man's Best Friend,* a series of directories that detail bed and breakfasts, inns, family resorts and other hotels/motels. Some places require a refundable deposit to cover any damage incurred by the dog. More B&Bs accept pets now, but some restrict the size.

If taking Rufus with you is not feasible, check out boarding kennels in your area. Your veterinarian may offer this service, or recommend a kennel or two he or she is familiar with. Go see the facilities for yourself, ask about exercise, diet, housing, and so on. Or, if you'd rather have Rufus stay home, look into bonded petsitters, many of whom will also bring in the mail and water your plants.

chapter 11

Your Dog and your Community

by Bardi McLennan

Step outside your home with your dog and you are no longer just family, you are both part of your community. This is when the phrase "responsible pet ownership" takes on serious implications. For starters, it means you pick up after your dog—not just occasionally, but every time your dog eliminates away from home. That means you have joined the Plastic Baggy Brigade! You always have plastic sandwich bags in your pocket and several in the car. It means you teach your kids how to use them, too. If you think this is "yucky," just imagine what the person (a non-doggy person) who inadvertently steps in the mess thinks!

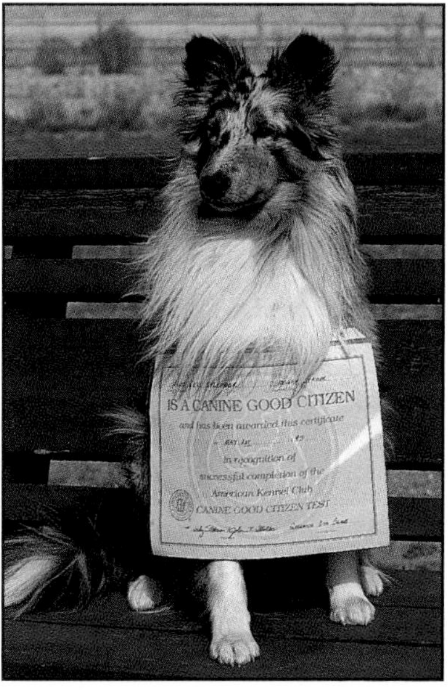

Your responsibility extends to your neighbors: To their ears (no annoying barking); to their property (their garbage, their lawn, their flower beds, their cat—especially their cat); to their kids (on bikes, at play); to their kids' toys and sports equipment.

There are numerous dog-related laws, ranging from simple dog licensing and leash laws to those holding you liable for any physical injury or property damage done by your dog. These laws are in place to protect everyone in the community, including you and your dog. There are town ordinances and state laws which are by no means the same in all towns or all states. Ignorance of the law won't get you off the hook. The time to find out what the laws are where you live is now.

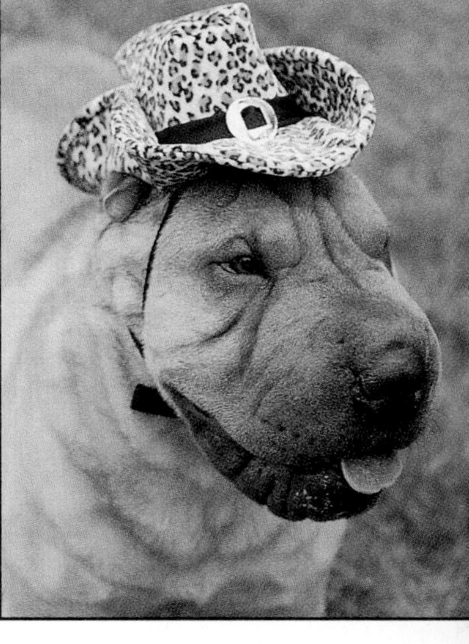

Dressing your dog up makes him appealing to strangers.

Be sure your dog's license is current. This is not just a good local ordinance, it can make the difference between finding your lost dog or not. Many states now require proof of rabies vaccination and that the dog has been spayed or neutered before issuing a license. At the same time, keep up the dog's annual immunizations.

Never let your dog run loose in the neighborhood. This will not only keep you on the right side of the leash law, it's the outdoor version of the rule about not giving your dog "freedom to get into trouble."

Good Canine Citizen

Sometimes it's hard for a dog's owner to assess whether or not the dog is sufficiently socialized to be accepted by the community at large. Does Rufus or Rufina display good, controlled behavior in public? The AKC's Canine Good Citizen program is available through many dog organizations. If your dog passes the test, the title "CGC" is earned.

The overall purpose is to turn your dog into a good neighbor and to teach you about your responsibility to your community as a dog owner. Here are the ten things your dog must do willingly:

1. Accept a stranger stopping to chat with you.
2. Sit and be petted by a stranger.
3. Allow a stranger to handle him or her as a groomer or veterinarian would.
4. Walk nicely on a loose lead.
5. Walk calmly through a crowd.
6. Sit and down on command, then stay in a sit or down position while you walk away.
7. Come when called.
8. Casually greet another dog.
9. React confidently to distractions.
10. Accept being left alone with someone other than you and not become overly agitated or nervous.

Schools and Dogs

Schools are getting involved with pet ownership on an educational level. It has been proven that children who are kind to animals are humane in their attitude toward other people as adults.

A dog is a child's best friend, and so children are often primary pet owners, if not the primary caregivers. Unfortunately, they are also the ones most often bitten by dogs. This occurs due to a lack of understanding that pets, no matter how sweet, cuddly and loving, are still animals. Schools, along with parents, dog clubs, dog fanciers and the AKC, are working to change all that with video programs for children not only in grade school, but in the nursery school and pre-kindergarten age group. Teaching youngsters how to be responsible dog owners is important community work. When your dog has a CGC, volunteer to take part in an educational classroom event put on by your dog club.

Boy Scout Merit Badge

A Merit Badge for Dog Care can be earned by any Boy Scout ages 11 to 18. The requirements are not easy, but amount to a complete course in responsible dog care and general ownership. Here are just a few of the things a Scout must do to earn that badge:

> Point out ten parts of the dog using the correct names.
>
> Give a report (signed by parent or guardian) on your care of the dog (feeding, food used, housing, exercising, grooming and bathing), plus what has been done to keep the dog healthy.
>
> Explain the right way to obedience train a dog, and demonstrate three comments.
>
> Several of the requirements have to do with health care, including first aid, handling a hurt dog, and the dangers of home treatment for a serious ailment.
>
> The final requirement is to know the local laws and ordinances involving dogs.

There are similar programs for Girl Scouts and 4-H members.

Local Clubs

Local dog clubs are no longer in existence just to put on a yearly dog show. Today, they are apt to be the hub of the community's involvement with pets. Dog clubs conduct educational forums with big-name speakers, stage demonstrations of canine talent in a busy mall and take dogs of various breeds to schools for classroom discussion.

The quickest way to feel accepted as a member in a club is to volunteer your services! Offer to help with something—anything—and watch your popularity (and your interest) grow.

Therapy Dogs

Once your dog has earned that essential CGC and reliably demonstrates a steady, calm temperament, you could look into what therapy dogs are doing in your area.

Therapy dogs go with their owners to visit patients at hospitals or nursing homes, generally remaining on leash but able to coax a pat from a stiffened hand, a smile from a blank face, a few words from sealed lips or a hug from someone in need of love.

Nursing homes cover a wide range of patient care. Some specialize in care of the elderly, some in the treatment of specific illnesses, some in physical therapy. Children's facilities also welcome visits from trained therapy dogs for boosting morale in their pediatric patients. Hospice care for the terminally ill and the at-home care of AIDS patients are other areas where this canine visiting is desperately needed. Therapy dog training comes first.

Your dog can make a difference in lots of lives.

There is a lot more involved than just taking your nice friendly pooch to someone's bedside. Doing therapy dog work involves your own emotional stability as well as that of your dog. But once you have met all the requirements for this work, making the rounds once a week or once a month with your therapy dog is possibly the most rewarding of all community activities.

Disaster Aid

This community service is definitely not for everyone, partly because it is time-consuming. The initial training is rigorous, and there can be no let-up in the continuing workouts, because members are on call 24 hours a day to go wherever they are needed at a moment's notice. But if you think you would like to be able to assist in a disaster, look into search-and-rescue work. The network of search-and-rescue volunteers is worldwide, and all members of the American Rescue Dog Association (ARDA) who are qualified to do this work are volunteers who train and maintain their own dogs.

Physical Aid

Making the rounds with your therapy dog can be very rewarding.

Most people are familiar with Seeing Eye dogs, which serve as blind people's eyes, but not with all the other work that dogs are trained to do to assist the disabled. Dogs are also specially trained to pull wheelchairs, carry school books, pick up dropped objects, open and close doors. Some also are ears for the deaf. All these assistance-trained dogs, by the way, are allowed anywhere "No Pet" signs exist (as are therapy dogs when properly identified). Getting started in any of this fascinating work requires a background in dog training and canine behavior, but there are also volunteer jobs ranging from answering the phone to cleaning out kennels to providing a foster home for a puppy. You have only to ask.

part four

Beyond the Basics

chapter 12

Recommended Reading

Books

About Health Care

Ackerman, Lowell. *Guide to Skin and Haircoat Problems in Dogs.* Loveland, Colo.: Alpine Publications, 1994.

Alderton, David. *The Dog Care Manual.* Hauppauge, N.Y.: Barron's Educational Series, Inc., 1986.

American Kennel Club. *American Kennel Club Dog Care and Training.* New York: Howell Book House, 1991.

Bamberger, Michelle, DVM. *Help! The Quick Guide to First Aid for Your Dog.* New York: Howell Book House, 1995.

Carlson, Delbert, DVM, and James Giffin, MD. *Dog Owner's Home Veterinary Handbook.* New York: Howell Book House, 1992.

DeBitetto, James, DVM, and Sarah Hodgson. *You & Your Puppy.* New York: Howell Book House, 1995.

Humphries, Jim, DVM. *Dr. Jim's Animal Clinic for Dogs.* New York: Howell Book House, 1994.

McGinnis, Terri. *The Well Dog Book.* New York: Random House, 1991.

Pitcairn, Richard and Susan. *Natural Health for Dogs.* Emmaus, Pa.: Rodale Press, 1982.

About Dog Shows

Hall, Lynn. *Dog Showing for Beginners.* New York: Howell Book House, 1994.

Nichols, Virginia Tuck. *How to Show Your Own Dog.* Neptune, N. J.: TFH, 1970.

Vanacore, Connie. *Dog Showing, An Owner's Guide.* New York: Howell Book House, 1990.

About Training

Ammen, Amy. *Training in No Time.* New York: Howell Book House, 1995.

Baer, Ted. *Communicating With Your Dog.* Hauppauge, N.Y.: Barron's Educational Series, Inc., 1989.

Benjamin, Carol Lea. *Dog Problems.* New York: Howell Book House, 1989.

Benjamin, Carol Lea. *Dog Training for Kids.* New York: Howell Book House, 1988.

Benjamin, Carol Lea. *Mother Knows Best.* New York: Howell Book House, 1985.

Benjamin, Carol Lea. *Surviving Your Dog's Adolescence.* New York: Howell Book House, 1993.

Bohnenkamp, Gwen. *Manners for the Modern Dog.* San Francisco: Perfect Paws, 1990.

Dibra, Bashkim. *Dog Training by Bash.* New York: Dell, 1992.

Dunbar, Ian, PhD, MRCVS. *Dr. Dunbar's Good Little Dog Book,* James & Kenneth Publishers, 2140 Shattuck Ave. #2406, Berkeley, Calif. 94704. (510) 658–8588. Order from the publisher.

Dunbar, Ian, PhD, MRCVS. *How to Teach a New Dog Old Tricks,* James & Kenneth Publishers. Order from the publisher; address above.

Dunbar, Ian, PhD, MRCVS, and Gwen Bohnenkamp. Booklets on *Preventing Aggression; Housetraining; Chewing; Digging; Barking; Socialization; Fearfulness; and Fighting,* James & Kenneth Publishers. Order from the publisher; address above.

Evans, Job Michael. *People, Pooches and Problems.* New York: Howell Book House, 1991.

Kilcommons, Brian and Sarah Wilson. *Good Owners, Great Dogs.* New York: Warner Books, 1992.

McMains, Joel M. *Dog Logic—Companion Obedience.* New York: Howell Book House, 1992.

Rutherford, Clarice and David H. Neil, MRCVS. *How to Raise a Puppy You Can Live With.* Loveland, Colo.: Alpine Publications, 1982.

Volhard, Jack and Melissa Bartlett. *What All Good Dogs Should Know: The Sensible Way to Train.* New York: Howell Book House, 1991.

About Breeding

Harris, Beth J. Finder. *Breeding a Litter, The Complete Book of Prenatal and Postnatal Care.* New York: Howell Book House, 1983.

Holst, Phyllis, DVM. *Canine Reproduction.* Loveland, Colo.: Alpine Publications, 1985.

Walkowicz, Chris and Bonnie Wilcox, DVM. *Successful Dog Breeding, The Complete Handbook of Canine Midwifery.* New York: Howell Book House, 1994.

About Activities

American Rescue Dog Association. *Search and Rescue Dogs.* New York: Howell Book House, 1991.

Barwig, Susan and Stewart Hilliard. *Schutzhund.* New York: Howell Book House, 1991.

Beaman, Arthur S. *Lure Coursing.* New York: Howell Book House, 1994.

Daniels, Julie. *Enjoying Dog Agility—From Backyard to Competition.* New York: Doral Publishing, 1990.

Davis, Kathy Diamond. *Therapy Dogs.* New York: Howell Book House, 1992.

Gallup, Davis Anne. *Running With Man's Best Friend.* Loveland, Colo.: Alpine Publications, 1986.

Habgood, Dawn and Robert. *On the Road Again With Man's Best Friend.* New England, Mid-Atlantic, West Coast and Southeast editions. Selective guides to area bed and breakfasts, inns, hotels and resorts that welcome guests and their dogs. New York: Howell Book House, 1995.

Holland, Vergil S. *Herding Dogs.* New York: Howell Book House, 1994.

LaBelle, Charlene G. *Backpacking With Your Dog.* Loveland, Colo.: Alpine Publications, 1993.

Simmons-Moake, Jane. *Agility Training, The Fun Sport for All Dogs.* New York: Howell Book House, 1991.

Spencer, James B. *Hup! Training Flushing Spaniels the American Way.* New York: Howell Book House, 1992.

Spencer, James B. *Point! Training the All-Seasons Birddog.* New York: Howell Book House, 1995.

Tarrant, Bill. *Training the Hunting Retriever.* New York: Howell Book House, 1991.

Volhard, Jack and Wendy. *The Canine Good Citizen.* New York: Howell Book House, 1994.

General Titles

Haggerty, Captain Arthur J. *How to Get Your Pet Into Show Business.* New York: Howell Book House, 1994.

McLennan, Bardi. *Dogs and Kids, Parenting Tips.* New York: Howell Book House, 1993.

Moran, Patti J. *Pet Sitting for Profit, A Complete Manual for Professional Success.* New York: Howell Book House, 1992.

Scalisi, Danny and Libby Moses. *When Rover Just Won't Do, Over 2,000 Suggestions for Naming Your Dog.* New York: Howell Book House, 1993.

Sife, Wallace, PhD. *The Loss of a Pet.* New York: Howell Book House, 1993.

Wrede, Barbara J. *Civilizing Your Puppy.* Hauppauge, N.Y.: Barron's Educational Series, 1992.

Magazines

The AKC GAZETTE, The Official Journal for the Sport of Purebred Dogs. American Kennel Club, 51 Madison Ave., New York, NY.

Bloodlines Journal. United Kennel Club, 100 E. Kilgore Rd., Kalamazoo, MI.

Dog Fancy. Fancy Publications, 3 Burroughs, Irvine, CA 92718

Dog World. Maclean Hunter Publishing Corp., 29 N. Wacker Dr., Chicago, IL 60606.

Videos

"SIRIUS Puppy Training," by Ian Dunbar, PhD, MRCVS. James & Kenneth Publishers, 2140 Shattuck Ave. #2406, Berkeley, CA 94704. Order from the publisher.

"Training the Companion Dog," from Dr. Dunbar's British TV Series, James & Kenneth Publishers. (See address above).

The American Kennel Club produces videos on every breed of dog, as well as on hunting tests, field trials and other areas of interest to purebred dog owners. For more information, write to AKC/Video Fulfillment, 5580 Centerview Dr., Suite 200, Raleigh, NC 27606.

chapter 13

Resources

Breed Clubs

Every breed recognized by the American Kennel Club has a national (parent) club. National clubs are a great source of information on your breed. You can get the name of the secretary of the club by contacting:

The American Kennel Club
51 Madison Avenue
New York, NY 10010
(212) 696-8200

There are also numerous all-breed, individual breed, obedience, hunting and other special-interest dog clubs across the country. The American Kennel Club can provide you with a geographical list of clubs to find ones in your area. Contact them at the above address.

Registry Organizations

Registry organizations register purebred dogs. The American Kennel Club is the oldest and largest in this country, and currently recognizes over 130 breeds. The United Kennel Club registers some breeds the AKC doesn't (including the American Pit Bull Terrier and the Miniature Fox Terrier) as well as many of the same breeds. The others included here are for your reference; the AKC can provide you with a list of foreign registries.

American Kennel Club
51 Madison Avenue
New York, NY 10010

United Kennel Club (UKC)
100 E. Kilgore Road
Kalamazoo, MI 49001-5598

American Dog Breeders Assn.
P.O. Box 1771
Salt Lake City, UT 84110
(Registers American Pit Bull Terriers)

Canadian Kennel Club
89 Skyway Avenue
Etobicoke, Ontario
Canada M9W 6R4

National Stock Dog Registry
P.O. Box 402
Butler, IN 46721
(Registers working stock dogs)

Orthopedic Foundation for Animals (OFA)
2300 E. Nifong Blvd.
Columbia, MO 65201-3856
(Hip registry)

Activity Clubs

Write to these organizations for information on the activities they sponsor.

American Kennel Club
51 Madison Avenue
New York, NY 10010
(Conformation Shows, Obedience Trials, Field Trials and Hunting Tests, Agility, Canine Good

Citizen, Lure Coursing, Herding, Tracking, Earthdog Tests, Coonhunting.)

United Kennel Club
100 E. Kilgore Road
Kalamazoo, MI 49001-5598
(Conformation Shows, Obedience Trials, Agility, Hunting for Various Breeds, Terrier Trials and more.)

North American Flyball Assn.
1342 Jeff St.
Ypsilanti, MI 48198

International Sled Dog Racing Assn.
P.O. Box 446
Norman, ID 83848-0446

North American Working Dog Assn., Inc.
Southeast Kreisgruppe
P.O. Box 833
Brunswick, GA 31521

Trainers

Association of Pet Dog Trainers
P.O. Box 3734
Salinas, CA 93912
(408) 663–9257

American Dog Trainers' Network
161 West 4th St.
New York, NY 10014
(212) 727–7257

National Association of Dog Obedience Instructors
2286 East Steel Rd.
St. Johns, MI 48879

Associations

American Dog Owners Assn.
1654 Columbia Tpk.
Castleton, NY 12033
(Combats anti-dog legislation)

Delta Society
P.O. Box 1080
Renton, WA 98057-1080
(Promotes the human/animal bond through pet-assisted therapy and other programs)

Dog Writers Assn. of America (DWAA)
Sally Cooper, Secy.
222 Woodchuck Ln.
Harwinton, CT 06791

National Assn. for Search and Rescue (NASAR)
P.O. Box 3709
Fairfax, VA 22038

Therapy Dogs International
6 Hilltop Road
Mendham, NJ 07945